The Librarian's

INTERNET SURVIVAL GUIDE

THE LIBRARIAN'S
INTERNET SURVIVAL GUIDE

STRATEGIES FOR THE HIGH-TECH REFERENCE DESK

Second Edition

Irene E. McDermott

Edited by
Barbara Quint

Information Today, Inc.

Medford, New Jersey

First printing, 2006

*The Librarian's Internet Survival Guide: Strategies for the High-Tech Reference Desk,
Second Edition*

Library of Congress Cataloging-in-Publication Data

McDermott, Irene E., 1959-
  The librarian's Internet survival guide : strategies for the high-tech
reference desk / by Irene E. McDermott ; edited by Barbara Quint.-- 2nd ed.
    p. cm.
  Includes bibliographical references and index.
  ISBN 1-57387-235-0
  1. Computer network resources--Directories. 2. Web sites--Directories. 3.
Internet in library reference services. 4. Internet--Handbooks, manuals,
etc. I. Quint, Barbara (Barbara E.), 1943- II. Title.
  ZA4225.M35 2005
  025.04--dc22

                                                                  2005030308

Printed and bound in the United States of America

President and CEO: Thomas H. Hogan, Sr.
Editor-in-Chief and Publisher: John B. Bryans
Managing Editor: Amy M. Reeve
VP Graphics and Production: M. Heide Dengler
Book Designer: Kara Mia Jalkowski
Cover Designer: Amanda Beland
Copyeditor: Pat Hadley-Miller
Proofreader: Kate Delaney
Indexer: Sharon Hughes

To Philip and Peter,
My guides to survival—with *style*.

Contents

Figures

Foreword

Although it seems a curious thing to admit in a foreword to a book about the Internet, I've always been a bit dubious about, well, books about the Internet. (And, yes, for those of you playing along at home, I've been involved in several. *Mea culpa*; I plead youthful exuberance.) I mean, look at some of the topics in this book: searchbots, blogs, aggregators, cascading style sheets, and so on. You could easily replace those with such mid-90s exotica as Gopher, archie, Veronica, finger, and this new thing called Mosaic, a "Web browser" that might be a big deal someday. Who knows how many of today's hot new things will still be around in a couple of years?

That's just the nature of the Web, of course; it's a dynamic, ever-changing place, but that doesn't necessarily mean that there's nothing more enduring or constant in that world.

As librarians, one of our central intellectual challenges today is figuring out how to use the Internet, and all that incorporates, without letting it overtake or overwhelm what is uniquely us. To me, that means: understanding what's there (and by extension, what's not), choosing as a result to use the free Internet when it's most appropriate or likely to be successful, finding and recognizing good stuff there, trying multiple approaches in that finding process, deciding when to stop or move on to more fruitful approaches, helping people to use and understand it, and other allied or related things.

What all that boils down to is adopting professional practice that we recognize as librarianship in a world that incorporates—one hesitates quite yet to say "is dominated by"—freely available Internet resources. As I write this, there is discussion, concern, and some consternation over recent announcements from Google: Google Book Search, Google Scholar, Desktop Search, local search, question-answering, and no doubt whatever gets announced tomorrow after I e-mail this to the publisher. Some of these will likely succeed and endure, others won't, and new things will continually come down the pike.

This is a big deal. If we can achieve this balance of professionalism and dynamism, we'll have moved a long way towards regaining a central position in the information lives of our communities, and make a difference in those lives. Because, frankly, we can't help anybody if they don't think of us as people who can help.

Irene's book can be an important part of that process. It's not just a reference book of good Web sites (thank heavens). She gets at process, technique, understanding—the kinds of higher-level stuff that distinguishes our profession.

In addition, the seemingly mundane is here as well—all the cool Web sites and search technology in the world won't help someone if the computer goes down, or their e-mail fails, or they can't access or understand what is there, and so on, and several chapters here address these critical if sometimes grubby and overlooked matters.

I applaud Irene and Barbara for their work on this book, and hope their readers—and, eventually, the wider public—profit from it.

Enjoy!

Joseph Janes
Seattle
May 2005

Joseph Janes is Associate Professor and Associate Dean for Academics at the Information School of the University of Washington. A frequent speaker in the U.S. and abroad, he was the Founding Director of the Internet Public Library and the co-author of eight books on librarianship, technology, and their relationship, including *Introduction to Reference Work in the Digital Age*, and writes the "Internet Librarian" column for *American Libraries* magazine. He holds an MLS and PhD from Syracuse University, and has taught at the University of Michigan, the University of North Carolina at Chapel Hill, the State University of New York at Albany, as well as at Syracuse and Washington.

Acknowledgments

I owe my biggest thanks to my editor, Barbara Quint. When she invited me to write a monthly column for her magazine in 1997, she gave me the opportunity not only to practice writing, but to have her as a mentor. Her guidance has been essential to me. It was she who proposed the idea to collect my columns in a book!

I am grateful also to my library director Carolyn Crain and my colleagues Rex Mayreis, Lynda Lyons, and Tara Smith, and all my other friends at the San Marino Public Library for their patience with me when my body was at the reference desk but my mind was contemplating deadlines.

I am deeply obliged to John B. Bryans, Amy Reeve, and the whole crew at Information Today. They certainly know how to make an author look good. Thanks also to John and Tom Hogan Sr. for believing in my book and publishing it.

I couldn't have gotten started on this whole Internet business if it hadn't been for my buddy Barbara Shepard, who offered me an internship at the Getty Research Institute in 1994, where I studied the baby Web. This valuable experience coincided with my time in the Masters of Library & Information Science (MLIS) program at the Department of Information Studies at UCLA, where Esther Grassian taught me how to teach. Thanks, Esther!

I want to recognize my former colleagues at Salem Press in Pasadena, especially Jim Magill, Dawn Dawson, and my boss-for-a-decade-yet-still-good-friend Jeff Jensen. You allowed me to earn a living while following my bliss.

Finally, I gratefully acknowledge the support of my husband Philip and my son, Peter James. As Shakespeare wrote, I love these guys "with so much of my heart that none is left to protest." They fill my life with every good thing.

How to Use This How-To Book

The Librarian's Internet Survival Guide is made up of chapters originally written as installments of my monthly column "Internet Express" for *Searcher* magazine. Of course, I did sneakily arrange in advance for the columns to add up to a collection. Now, revised, expanded, and updated, each chapter is written to stand on its own, as it did when it originally appeared in the magazine.

This leaves the reader with a choice about how to use this book. You can, of course, sit down and read it all the way through. Still, it might be more useful to turn to each chapter as you need it.

The first nine chapters offer sites that the high-tech reference desk could use to answer patron questions. For example, Chapter 1 explores metasearch engines. Although these may not be the most precise way to search the Web, they are certainly the most comprehensive.

Use Chapter 2 to help those patrons looking for ancestors, lost loves, or just people who owe them money. Chapter 3, "News on the Net," is for those obsessed with current events. Here, I address the usefulness of "blogs" as well as news aggregators that use RSS technology.

Chapter 4 offers quality Web resources suitable for study or other work in which accuracy is critical. The sites in Chapter 5 are aimed at the younger set. Some are for school; others are just for fun. I also address fears that parents may have about the safety of their young ones in cyberspace.

Chapter 6, "Free Full-Text Resources," can help students who have to read "classics" (books published before 1923) that may be missing from the library shelves. Turn to this chapter, too, when patrons need information from the federal government. The Feds not only funded the early Internet, but in fact, the Web increasingly has become the Federal government's preferred "digital" printer (they have published many resources on the Web and offer them free for the taking).

The information in Chapter 7, about medical resources, is known to have saved at least one life. At the very least, it can arm patrons with basic knowledge of their illnesses so they can have informed conversations with their doctors—and their health insurance companies.

Increase your capital with the sites in Chapter 8. The stock market was flying high when I originally wrote this chapter. After that, it slumped and then recovered somewhat. It also got blasted by scandal, e.g., the collapse of Enron. Still, the basic personal financial advice offered by the sites in this chapter remains sound. There is even a bit about how to detect fraud in a company that you might see as a potential investment opportunity.

If patrons take this advice and consequently have money to spend, point them to Chapter 9 for Internet shopping resources. Not only will they find the best prices, they can get reviews to help them choose the most reliable products.

The final six chapters of the book are aimed at those of us on the other side of the high-tech reference desk. As librarians, we are responsible for providing access to electronic information. Part of that duty entails teaching the Internet to our patrons, placing us in the uncomfortable position of offering bibliographic instruction (Chapter 11) in a medium that we may not understand very well ourselves! We can produce our own Web "pathfinders" (Chapter 12) to help our lessons stick. We can even share our information with disabled people over the Web if we use those newfangled Cascading Style Sheets, or CSS (Chapter 13).

At the high-tech reference desk, we can expect to be asked to help patrons manage their e-mail and fix minor computer glitches (Chapter 10 and Chapter 14) in addition to regular information questions. And we can look forward to performing basic maintenance on our own library computers.

Finally, Chapter 15 offers tools to help us keep our nails dug in to that protean beast that is the World Wide Web. No matter what shape it takes as it evolves, for us librarians, the Internet will continue to be a useful tool in our information arsenal.

I wrote this book directly from my own experience of everyday interactions at the high-tech reference desk at the San Marino Public Library. I don't even pretend to cover every situation a librarian might encounter—but I hope I've given you enough to survive on!

The Magic Answer Machine

Guess who became a knight? Tim Berners-Lee, the inventor of the World Wide Web (http://news.bbc.co.uk/1/hi/technology/3899723.stm). Berners-Lee, or "Sir Tim" as he is now known, thought up the idea of hyperlinks, the basis of the World Wide Web, in 1990. By 1994, the graphical version of his concept sparked a revolution in information delivery that utterly changed the way libraries do business.

At the time, some predicted that the Web would make libraries obsolete. In fact, just the opposite happened. "Visits to public libraries have more than doubled to 1.2 billion annually in the past 12 years, and many of these people are coming for computer and Internet access," declared Carol Brey Casiano, president of American Library Association (ALA) at the group's June 2005 conference (www.ala.org/ala/pressreleases2005/june2004abc/libraries computeraccess.htm).

That's just great. Still, we have to wonder: Do our new patrons love us for our brains or our machines?

Offering free Internet access in libraries has caused a few headaches. For one thing, we have to buy computers, which are expensive. They need constant maintenance and frequent replacement. They put a tremendous strain on tight library budgets. Our resources are finite, yet the public demand for Internet access seems insatiable. We will never be able to provide enough computers to satisfy our patrons, and the ones we have will always be out of date.

Our professional mandate as librarians is to offer fair access to the Web to everyone. But because the Web is addictive and wild, we end up having to devote a lot of energy deciding who may use our computers to access the Web, how long they may use them, and often times, what they may view. Every day, when my library opens, the men (mostly) rush to take their usual seats in front of our computers, where they resemble nothing so much as bar flies. By implication, doesn't that mean that we are little more than bartenders of the World Wide Web?

Despite the problems that stem from offering the Internet to the public, the Web remains the reference librarian's best friend. I know that I use it as my personal magic answer machine. As the technology sector of the economy regains its vigor, more electronic resources come online. The recent rise of the open source movement has put high-quality scholarly information at our fingertips. Now, the amazing Google plans to place the entire text of scholarly tomes online for free, much to the chagrin of publishers.

I have written this book to help us take advantage of all that Internet goodness out there, while dealing with the problems that Web access brings to libraries.

I do not address the tough issues that librarians must decide for themselves, with input from their communities and system administrators. These include funding for Internet access, acceptable use policies, system security, printing options, multimedia use in the library, Internet privacy, and pornography. There are no universal "right" ways to manage these challenges. Often, the best way is to craft admittedly imperfect policies, compromises that seem the least "wrong" for a community culture.

I have faith that new technologies will soon relieve some of the infrastructure and control issues that come with offering public Internet access in libraries today. In the near future, all libraries will provide Wi-Fi access to the Web. As patrons bring their own laptops and Web-enabled mobile phones into our buildings, librarians will become increasingly liberated from the burden of computer repair, something for which we were never trained and that we do only reluctantly. We will still have to keep a few public access machines around for travelers or the home technology-challenged. Still, we will spend much less time rebooting computers, leaving us the leisure to teach our patrons how to separate the hearty, wheat-ful Web sites from the trashy chaff. In other words, through this technology, we reference librarians will reach ever higher peaks of productivity and indispensability. As Barbara Quint, information visionary and editor of this book says, "We may not always need libraries, but we will always need librarians!"

Part 1

Ready Reference on the Web: Resources for Patrons

Quick! What is the best Web resource for finding a good vacuum cleaner? Getting information for a grade-school "state" report? Finding a life-saving clinical trial?

People just walk up to our desks and ask us these questions every day. And we are expected to answer them in seconds, not minutes or hours.

For heaven's sake! How are *we* supposed to know?

As Robert W. Winter, Arthur G. Coons Professor of the History of Ideas, Emeritus at Occidental College in Los Angeles, once told our class, "A liberal arts education will teach you what you don't know." In other words, as educated people, as *librarians*, we know that we don't know everything, yet we are armed with tools to find out about anything.

My hope is that the first section of this book can serve as one of those tools. I have tried to cover some of the most asked subject areas that I encounter every day on the job. I also point to directories of high-quality sites that can quickly connect librarians and their patrons to the answers that they need.

These listings may not answer every question. But I guarantee you, if you can learn to turn to them first, your patrons will hail your alacrity and brilliance.

And isn't this glory what we librarians *live* for?

Chapter 1

Searching and Metasearching the Internet

The topic of searching the Web puts me in an elegiac mood. I think back to 1994 when I was first playing with the Web during my library school internship at the Getty Research Institute. For 15 hours every week, I scrolled and clicked, calling in new home pages from around the world. My desk faced a window seven stories above the Santa Monica Bay, with its whitecaps and sailboats and Catalina Island in the distance. Yet, I found the baby Web so arresting that I rarely looked up from my task to admire the view.

In that year, Yahoo! (www.yahoo.com) was just a little hyperlinked directory maintained by a couple of guys from Stanford University. The search engine of choice was Lycos (www.lycos. com), which seemed at the time to be a marvel of software engineering, able to find anything that existed on that sparsely populated World Wide Web. Later, Lycos foundered, started selling its listings, and lost its edge to such newer engines as Infoseek and AltaVista (www.altavista.com). Now, Lycos is back, Infoseek is gone, and AltaVista is a fading presence bought by the "paid listing" search engine called Overture, which was subsequently purchased by Yahoo!.

Yes, even as the seasons change, so do the search engines. Disney bought Infoseek, renamed it GO.com (www.go.com), and turned it into a portal for Disney press releases. Another search engine, FAST Search's AllTheWeb.com (www.alltheweb.com), appeared and purported to index more Web pages than anyone else—until it too was purchased by Yahoo!.

7

Amid all this chaos of bursting and fading search tools, two Stanford PhD candidates, Larry Page and Sergey Brin, came up with a technologically advanced method to analyze links on Web pages. In 1998, they applied their paradigm through a new search engine called Google (www.google.com). It became an instant success, famed for both the simplicity of its interface and the almost spooky relevance of its results. Google bases its relevancy rankings on a complex network of algorithms, including a popularity factor determined by the number of links pointing to a site. It also considers the importance, based on linkage, of the pages pointing to the site. The result, especially for common word searches, is spectacular and highly resistant to "spamdexing." (Spamdexing is the application of false or misleading metatags to Web content designed to highjack searchers to the spamdexer's site. It corresponds to sending unwanted messages via e-mail, a.k.a. spam, and constitutes a serious problem for search engines, so much so that the struggle between spamdexers and search engines is referred to as an "arms race.")

Of course, Google's relevance comes at a price. Its default Boolean "AND" cuts out many results. Admittedly, many of those results would have been irrelevant. Still, Google might miss obscure sites that contain rare treasures.

Because of its honing features, Google is a great library assistant if you need precise results from the Internet. Not too long ago a patron came up to the reference desk and asked if we had that book by, "… oh, you know, that lawyer in the O.J. trial, the one that always wears buckskin."

I knew exactly who he was talking about. I could see the man's face doing lawyerly analysis on TV. But danged if I could remember the guy's name. So I pulled up Google and typed "lawyer O.J. buckskin" into the search box. "Gerry Spence" came up in the first hit. Holy cow!

Google is also great for finding poems based on half-remembered lines quoted by patrons. "I want that poem that starts with 'I have slipped the surly bonds of earth,'" a patron will ask. Imagine using a book to find the first line of a poem for which you have no frame of reference. But type "I have slipped the surly bonds of earth" into the Google search box (enclosing the phrase in quotation marks), and up pops the text of the poem "High Flight" by John Gillespie Magee Jr., who was killed in World War II during a dogfight at age 19. Just what our patrons asked for!

Google has all kinds of tricks, and it keeps getting better. Google's Local Search (http://local.google.com/lochp) will graphically point out categories of businesses in the user-specified vicinity for Canada, the U.S., and the U.K. At the results screen, click the "Map" button for a map or directions to a chosen business. Or click the "Sat" button for a satellite view from about 3,000 feet high.

For more fun, PC users can download "Google Earth," the updated and expanded version of its Keyhole 3D satellite imagery acquisition. Users can "fly" over a route to a destination, or just sightsee interesting points on our world. The basic application is free. More detailed images are available for a fee.

Both Google and Yahoo! will search a version of the Online Computer Library Center (OCLC) union catalog, called Open WorldCat, for books held in OCLC libraries near you. Type "find in a library" in quotation marks or site:worldcatlibraries.org in the Google search box along with the bibliographic information for the book you seek. Results will tell you which OCLC libraries near you hold the title.

Figure 1.1   With Google Local, get your results on a map or a satellite image.

Beyond Google: Other Search Engines and Web Directories

Google may be king, but there are other search engines out there that use different ranking and indexing methods. These search engines may yield different yet strong results that can complement a Google search.

Yahoo!
www.yahoo.com

Yahoo!, the Web's first major search engine, has been on a buying spree. When it purchased Overture in 2003, Yahoo! acquired both of the search engines that Overture had bought the year before: AltaVista and AllTheWeb. Yahoo! also bought Inktomi and then combined the search strategies of all these acquisitions to make the current potent Yahoo! search engine.

Yahoo!'s portal page is chockablock with a variety of news, ads, and links to other services. For a clean page that offers only search, go to Yahoo! Search (http://search.yahoo.com).

Yahoo!'s results formerly came from its directory of handpicked entries. That directory is still available at the Yahoo! Search Directory (http://dir.yahoo.com). Think of it as "Yahoo! Classic."

Yahoo! offers a powerful search toolbar that works with Internet Explorer. It allows users to customize the buttons on the appliance, giving users one-click links to their favorite information. The toolbar also blocks those annoying advertising pop-ups and features an anti-spyware search feature. Yahoo! recently teamed up with OCLC to offer a specialized toolbar that lets users search the Open WorldCat version of OCLC's union catalog. Download this integrated library search application at OCLC (www.oclc.org/toolbar) or simply type "find in a library" before bibliographic information in the Yahoo! search box. The result, from worldcatlibraries.org, can tell you which OCLC libraries near you hold the book that you seek.

Yahoo! continues to expand its search base with its "Content Acquisition Program." This involves not only indexing more commercial sites, but also expanding its ability to search databases, a.k.a. the "Invisible Web."

Finally, like Google, Yahoo! has added a search interface to find local business and services (www.yahoo.com). Although it lacks Google's satellite view feature, its results seem to be more accurate and relevant than its rival's.

Open Directory
http://dmoz.org

Talk about your "handpicked"! Here is the Web's largest human-edited directory, compiled entirely by volunteers. Its listings also power the Google Directory (www.google.com/dirhp). Actually, Google technology makes searching the directory a lot more relevant and useful. If you can't find what you need at the original site, visit the Google page.

AskJeeves

www.ask.com

Many nonlibrarians will turn to AskJeeves' friendly interface because it appears to answer questions phrased in "natural language," or in other words, "How do I take care of tortoise eggs?" instead of "tortoise eggs care." Web results come from the Teoma search engine, a smaller but highly relevant application that AskJeeves bought in 2001.

Gigablast

www.gigablast.com

This svelte search engine is entirely engineered by one person. Matt Wells wanted to take on Google by using a much lighter infrastructure. Gigablast generates highly relevant results and offers related search terms called "Giga Bits."

All these engines are terrific in themselves. Still, wouldn't it be great if you could search them all at once, without having to bounce from portal to portal? Well you can, if you use a metasearch engine.

Metasearch Sites

Web sites that access several search engines from one place or at one search command have been around for a while. They're a great idea, really, but they haven't been that practical. Some sites force users to search one engine at a time, the only advantage being that users don't have to retype their search terms. Others will parallel search several engines, but will not "de-dupe," that is, remove duplicate results. Then, of course, the user ends up with a huge result set full of repeats. Bummer.

But now, like the Web itself, some metasearch sites are maturing. Here are some of the best. Which one you use depends on the features you like the most.

Vivísimo

http://vivisimo.com

Scientists at Carnegie Mellon University conspired to cook up this metasearch engine that de-dupes, parses, and clusters results. The result display offers two parallel frames: One page frame holds general results and another lists subject clusters. Choose the cluster most relevant to your query to be rewarded with a nest of appropriate results. Vivísimo queries many engines at the same time, then delivers search results that are the cream of the crop. Another virtue—it doesn't search engines in which advertisers pay to be listed. Vivísimo is great for finding that obscure piece of information while bypassing ads.

Dogpile

www.dogpile.com

What a cute little puppy! And a fine metasearch engine, too. It automatically searches Google, Yahoo!, AskJeeves, About.com, and others for Web pages, images, or multimedia files. Use the Advanced Search feature to apply Boolean terms or impose filters by language, domain, or adult content. The results are sorted by individual search engine results. Good dog!

Ixquick

www.ixquick.com

David Bodnick has created this most technologically sophisticated of metasearch engines. It is one of the few metasearch tools that can understand both natural language and advanced Boolean searches and knows which engines can handle what syntax. It ranks its results by relevance and gives details about the ranking in the engines it queries. Search the Web, or just search news, images, or MP3 music. Try your search in English, German, Spanish, French, Italian, Dutch, or Portuguese.

Mama Metasearch
www.mamma.com

We know that the words of Saddam Hussein have indeed entered our lexicon when a metasearch utility calls itself "The Mother of All Search Engines." The simple interface searches the top engines and directories. Try the "Power Search" to pick and choose among the resources and add content filters.

KartOO.com
www.kartoo.com

How cool is this? KartOO not only does a metasearch, it displays the results as a Macromedia Flash information map. See how your search results relate to each other—literally.

Karnak Library
www.karnak.com

So you've got a lot of work to do on a long-term project. Register at the Karnak Library and have it leisurely search the Web. It will e-mail its results to you within 8 to 20 minutes. For monthly fees ranging from $10 to $75, Karnak will store your search results on its server, allowing access from wherever you log on. It also serves as

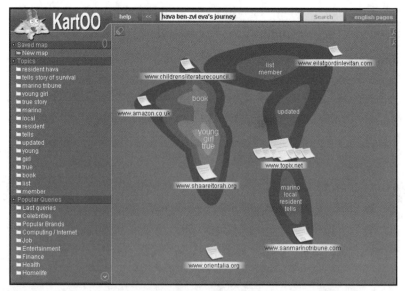

Figure 1.2   See your search results laid out in graphical format at KartOO.

a current awareness service that notifies you when new results appear. If you need in-depth results and have time to wait, this is the metaresearch tool for you.

Search the Invisible Web

Not all Web-enabled data is lying out there in HTML format. Much information lies concealed in databases (like telephone directories) or in collections of .pdf files (written in Adobe Acrobat, www.adobe.com). In the past, regular search engines have not been able to mine this data; it was "invisible" to them. That is changing as the engines become more sophisticated. For example, mighty Google now searches 12 file formats, including PDF documents, Microsoft Office, MS Word, PostScript, Corel WordPerfect, and Lotus 1-2-3. Some specialized services fashion their directories especially to access obscure gems.

CompletePlanet
http://aip.completeplanet.com

Want to know what's on the "Deep" or "Invisible" Web? CompletePlanet offers this list of subject-specific search engines and searchable databases. An advanced search page offers Boolean narrowing and searches by field and date. This is a very deep and complete search resource.

OAIster
http://oaister.umdl.umich.edu/o/oaister

The University of Michigan's Digital Library Production Service has developed a proprietary "middleware" application that performs real-time searches of academic databases invisible to regular search engines. This makes OAIster a virtual unified search interface of open archive, high-quality articles and Web sites from almost 400 academic institutions around the world. Browse institutional databases by title or search the whole danged thing in a delineated field search or by keyword.

Google Scholar
http://scholar.google.com

"Stand on the shoulders of giants" reads the tag line for this beta Google search service. Google Scholar combs peer-reviewed journals, books, abstracts, preprints, theses, and technical reports—in other words, scholarly information available across the Web from all areas of research. Relevance ranking on Google Scholar takes into account not only the full text of each piece but also how often it has been cited in academic literature. It will even locate scholarly books in nearby libraries through a connection to OCLC's Open WorldCat.

Browser Searchbots for the Desktop

Maybe now you are so excited by metasearching that you want to do it from your desktop! Here are a couple of outstanding freeware programs that allow users to search many engines at once.

Copernic Meta
www.copernic.com

Copernic Meta, offered by Copernic Technologies Inc., comes in two flavors: a Windows "Deskbar" that tucks itself into your Windows taskbar and a "Toolbar" designed to work with Microsoft Internet Explorer. Meta performs searches of up to 80 search engines in seven categories. Seconds after you have launched a search, it will start to display results on the screen as it finds them, without duplicates, then sorted in relevance order. Go ahead and use fuzzy Boolean. It lets you know which of the engines you picked doesn't support that feature. There is a commercial package as well as a free version.

WebFerret
www.ferretsoft.com

WebFerret searches several major engines and de-dupes the results quickly and simply. Pro: It can also search the news. Con: It doesn't search Google.

Keeping Up with the Engines

As the Internet is always in flux, so are the search engines. Where can you go to keep pace with the engines?

Search Engine Watch
http://searchenginewatch.com

Fortunately, there is a fellow who makes it his job to stay on top of the changes. His name is Danny Sullivan, and you are probably familiar with his site, Search Engine Watch. Sullivan covers everything remotely search-engine related, including techniques for successfully submitting your own site to the engines. He even covers specialized search engines, those tuned to certain subjects such as news, shopping, children, medicine, legal topics, and the Invisible Web. Read his monthly Search Engine Report for free, or subscribe to more in-depth information at the site for $99 per year. Sullivan's reports are also available via RSS feed.

SearchDay Newsletter
www.searchenginewatch.com/searchday

Chris Sherman, associate editor of Search Engine Watch and author of several books, including *Google Power* (McGraw-Hill

Figure 1.3   Keep up with changing search tools at Search Engine Watch.

Osborne Media, 2004, ISBN 0072257873), keeps users informed about Web-searching trends in a friendly, companionable way. Sign up at http://searchenginewatch.com/sereport.

Search Engine Showdown
www.searchengineshowdown.com

Research librarian Greg R. Notess offers analyses of search engines, including charts showing their relative strengths and weaknesses. He points the way to several subject-specific engines and offers searching tips to get the most out of all of them. Breaking news from Notess is available via RSS feed. This is a great site for the analytically inclined.

Searching Rule of Thumb

Sometimes, what we want to find on the Web just isn't there or isn't listed in a search engine. For example, our city manager once asked me to find her daughter's soccer schedule on the Internet. She had seen the URL on a sign at the playing field; she knew it existed. But I looked for an hour and still couldn't find it.

Whether we use Google or the most powerful metasearch engine, a good rule of thumb for both our patrons and ourselves is to devote no more than 20 minutes to any search. If we can't locate the page we want on the Web within that time, it probably isn't there. Or maybe it just hasn't been written properly, with powerful metatags that attract search engines. In any case, it's out of our control. This can be hard to explain to our patrons, who think that everything is easily accessible on the Web—or should be.

The city manager returned to her daughter's soccer field, and this time she wrote down the URL on the sign. Sure enough, it pulled up the Web page that gave her the information she wanted. I felt especially embarrassed because I, supposedly the searching expert, was unable to fulfill my city manager's simple request. Oh well, we can't win them all!

Chapter 2

Using the Web to Find People

Put two-dozen strangers in a room. Tell them to turn to their neighbor and ask, "What do you want most?" After they get an answer, have them ask another stranger, then another. Within five minutes, the whole room will be sobbing, racked with longing and heartbreak, pining for absent friends, family, colleagues—even enemies.

Great party game, huh? But it's true. Our dearest fantasies—to bring back lost loved ones—are so powerful that we dare not look at them too often. "Life is a series of meetings and partings. That is the way of it," wrote Charles Dickens. One of the hardest lessons of living is learning to accept loss.

Still, I often wish that I could talk with childhood friends that I once loved so much. I'd like to know more about my ancestors, too. For instance, all I know about my grandmother, my dad's mom, is that she died young, on Christmas Eve when my father was a child. She was a diabetic, and a neighbor brought over a holiday tin full of fudge. She said, "I'm going to eat this fudge if it kills me." It did. As she died, dogs howled, and she gasped, "Take care of my children!" All five of them. No wonder my dad never liked Christmas.

Am I wrong, or is this a gothic tale of suicide by chocolate? When did this happen? Did it *really* happen? And what about that ridiculous name of hers, "Orpha Esta," that my dad claimed came from the Bible. What is the truth of my family history?

Patrons and professionals alike have family stories with intriguing blank spots, as well as internal dramas of friends and lovers lost. Or, maybe we just want to trace that bum who scammed us out of our cabin rent deposit so we can serve him a summons for small claims court. Either way, the Web has become a powerful and popular tool for finding people. Private investigators grumble that online search services are taking away much of their business: The databases that were once their private domain are now publicly accessible over the Internet. Some longtime professional searchers know exactly how they feel.

What kind of information is out there, where do you find it, and how much does it cost? Many Web sites offer searchable telephone directories online, both national and international. Also, U.S. vital records are becoming more freely available online. RootsWeb, for example, offers searchable California death records from 1940 through 1997 (http://vitals.rootsweb.com/ca/death/search.cgi).

Many states are making professional license information freely available. This allows patrons to check that their doctor, lawyer, or cosmetologist is currently licensed to practice in their state, and whether he or she has a clean record.

What *is* restricted, or what will cost money, are the in-depth "background checks." These include credit reports, driving and criminal records, and bankruptcy and lawsuit information. Access to marriage and divorce records also usually entails a fee, as do asset searches, that is, listings of real estate, watercraft, and aircraft ownership.

Still, that doesn't mean that all of our personal information is just hanging out there. Privacy laws are getting tighter—and for good reason. Remember the murder of actress Rebecca Schaeffer by Robert John Bardo, a crazed fan, in 1989? Bardo said that he was inspired by the ease with which the 1982 attacker of actress Theresa Saldana got that victim's address. Bardo hired a private detective to find Schaeffer. His Tucson-based P.I. obtained the actress's home address from the California Department of Motor Vehicles for a fee of $4. In response to the murder, California lawmakers greatly restricted access to motor vehicle records, restricting the database to law enforcement officials and lawyers only.

Free Telephone and Address Directories

Helping patrons locate people and businesses got much easier with the advent of online telephone directories. The contents of hundreds of those huge floppy yellow and white pages are now freely available on the Web. Directory coverage is not limited to the U.S. and Canada; many other nations have put their phone books online, too. One of my patrons just used the public access computers in our library to find the phone number and address of her second cousin in Armenia!

What are the restrictions? These directories include only published or listed phone numbers. Also, the information in these databases may be incorrect or out-of-date. There is no easy, free way to find fax, pager, or cell phone numbers. However, Web phone directory sites often offer toll-free "800" number searches and reverse directories; that is, they allow the user to type in a phone number to find the name connected with it.

For the U.S. and Canada, there are a lot of free directory information sites on the Web. Yet every one of these directories buys almost all of its data from one of the first two information aggregator companies listed here. The others offer a variety of value-added search functions, such as being able to scour the entire nation for a business or personal name with one click.

Acxiom Corporation
www.acxiom.com/default.aspx

Where does "Information" get its information? Who puts the "ID" in "Caller ID"? Acxiom Corporation, that's who. Acxiom's "InfoBase" is a residential and business telephone and address database with more than 123 million telephone and address listings throughout the United States and 16 million Canadian listings. Web sites that use Acxiom's database include Verizon's SuperPages.com (www.superpages.com), Lycos (www.lycos.com; www.whowhere. com), and InfoSpace.com (www. infospace.com).

InfoUSA
www.infousa.com

InfoUSA is Acxiom's main rival in the directory database business. Its telephone directory search page, called Directory Assistance Plus (www.daplus.us), will search for people, businesses, yellow pages categories, and even reverse telephone lookups.

SuperPages.com
http://superpages.com

Verizon's interface makes it easy to search the nation for people or businesses listed in telephone directories. Use their "Global Directories" link to find directories from around the globe.

The Ultimates
http://theultimates.com

Scott Martin has assembled pages that allow the user to type in a name once and then run it through several directories (with perhaps the same basic databases, but with different search features)

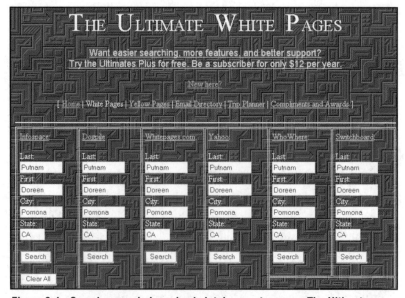

Figure 2.1   Search several phone book databases at once on The Ultimates.

without having to retype. The search boxes all appear on one page, but each search opens a new results window.

Nedsite
www.nedsite.nl/search/people.htm

Nedsite, an Amsterdam-based Internet portal, boasts no directory information of its own. Instead, it has assembled a long list of links to the world's phone, fax, and e-mail directories on the Web. It includes special sections for classmate searches, military directories, missing person searches, and genealogy resources.

E-Mail Search

Most of the telephone directory Web sites also offer e-mail address searches; a few directories and engines search for e-mail addresses exclusively. Newsgroup archives and class reunion sites offer an indirect avenue of locating e-mail addresses. Of course, the best way to get someone's e-mail address is just to call the person and ask. But where's the fun in that?

MESA: Your MetaEmailSearchAgent
http://mesa.rrzn.uni-hannover.de

This German site offers the largest e-mail address book worldwide. Search Suchen.de, IAF, SwissInfo, Yahoo! People Search, and Bigfoot in parallel. After 30 seconds, MESA will give you a clear report of its search results, along with links to the search engines. Once you get there, you must repeat the search, but at least you know the site has the information. Compliments to the Computer Center of Lower Saxony at the University of Hanover for coming up with such a handy service.

Google Groups
http://groups-beta.google.com

This is the Usenet database formerly known as Deja.com. Google is the knight in shining armor that rescued it and added some fabulous search functionality. Search Google Groups for the name of a friend or relative. Who knows? You might get lucky and pull up an e-mail address.

Classmates.com
www.classmates.com

Register for free, then look and see who else has registered from your high school, college, or even elementary school class. If you find someone, you can pay a fee, then send them an e-mail message and get back in touch—that is, if you actually want to talk to those people you may never have really liked, even back then. This site also features searches for old work pals, a military search, and will even search for classmates from schools across the world.

Finding Family

If anything fascinates humans as much as finding living loved ones, it's digging up information about ancestors. Somehow, discovering details about our roots helps us to understand who we are, to feel our place in the world, and maybe to understand peculiar behaviors in ourselves that turn out to be inherited. (My grandfather was a picky eater and my uncle was duck-toed, which explains a couple of things about me!) Our patrons who are fascinated by genealogy are in luck, because more and more personal historical records are coming online.

Family trees on the Web have been grassroots affairs, assembled and mounted by interested volunteers. The Church of Jesus Christ of Latter Day Saints has been a major collector of genealogical information, due to their belief that the dead can be baptized into the Mormon faith by proxy. They have made much of their collected research available to the public. Many local governments in the U.S. have begun to index their vital records in electronic format, perfect for putting up on the Web.

So many people use the Web to search old databases for traces of their ancestors that many of these services now charge subscription fees. Still, some remain free for the searching. Following are some free and fee places for finding family members from the past.

American Family Immigration History Center
www.ellisisland.org

Search the Ellis Island archives to find ancestors that passed through this New York immigrant processing center between 1892 and 1924. Search by name, year of arrival, age at arrival, gender, ethnicity, and port of departure.

FamilySearch Internet Genealogy Service
www.familysearch.org

The Mormon Church provides this portal for searching their vast genealogical record collections. The site also offers tips for building a family tree.

Social Security Death Index
http://ssdi.genealogy.rootsweb.com

Even though RootsWeb.com is a commercial service, it offers this portal for searching the Social Security Death Index (SSDI) for free. The SSDI database covers deceased people who lived after the inauguration of Social Security in the 1930s and earned benefits. Not all the deceased who carried Social Security cards will appear on the SSDI. The Index lists only those people for whom the government paid a lump sum death benefit. Still, if the database has the dead person whom you seek, you'll find out a lot about them here, including their social security number, date of birth, month and year of death, and city of last residence or payment. Entries link to a printable form letter that makes it easy for users to obtain copies of the deceased's original social security card application.

GeneaNet: Genealogical Database Network
www.geneanet.org

GeneaNet aims to compile a universal register of all the world's genealogical databases both free and fee-based. Free registration buys access to most of the site's features, although advanced and federated search features require payment of a subscription fee. This is a great site for international searches.

MyFamily.com
www.myfamily.com

This Provo, Utah-based commercial site owns Ancestry.com, RootsWeb.com, Genealogy.com, and Ancestry.co.uk. It features space to build your own family Web site for annual fees ranging from $30 to $210.

Public Records

Public records are just that—public. Governments make these available to anyone who wants to see them. In the past, searchers usually had to show up in person, sift through records themselves, then pay a fee to copy the ones they wanted. Having public records online is a tremendous time-saver. Searchers can now use the Web to discover all kinds of wild things about people: whether they have declared bankruptcy; if they own a home and, if so, where; and whether they have a professional license registered with the state. Are they married? Have they been divorced? Been convicted of a felony? Check out prospective employees—or a blind date! Note: Many public records can only be accessed through a commercial service for a fee. There are some, though, that float right out there on the open Web.

Search Systems
www.searchsystems.net

Pacific Information Resources, Inc. offers a directory of links to more than 21,000 searchable, freely accessible public record databases in the United States, Canada, and the rest of the world.

Free Public Records Sites
www.brbpub.com/pubrecsites.asp

BRB Publications, Inc., home of the "Public Record Research Library," offers links to state, county, city, federal (court), and important nongovernment sites where users can search public record information for free. It does not include information for state occupational licensing boards or registrations.

Background Checks that Cost Money

Caveat, searcher! Database producers can have a wide array of pricing for access to their people-information databases. Producers often distribute information through several routes, and prices may vary substantially from one outlet to the next. For example, one vendor may charge you $95 for a search, while another outlet would charge $5 or less a pop. As information professionals, we are responsible for finding the best deal for the best information retrieved as quickly as possible. This is one area where it pays to shop around, particularly when much of the commercial material is based on public domain records that some governments offer on the Web for free.

Still, if you've combed the free databases and have not found what you need, you might want to run a check through a fee-based service. Here are some of the best.

KnowX
www.knowx.com

Now owned by ChoicePoint (see page 28), this reputable service offers comprehensive people search results for reasonable prices. KnowX allows users to search its "Ultimate People Finder" database for free. I use it as a nationwide search. Once you determine in what state a lost one may reside, proceed to telephone directories to get direct contact information. KnowX is a terrific starting point.

Intelius People Search
http://find.intelius.com

This new people-finding service was founded after 9/11 by a group of senior executives and technologists from InfoSpace and Microsoft,

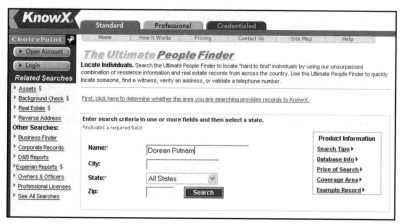

Figure 2.2 **Do a nationwide search of public records and get hit results free on KnowX.com.**

primarily, it seems, to help the government track terrorists. Their slogan? "We know." As a side benefit, the public may search their database for free. Buy a day pass to view in-depth information for about $20.

ChoicePoint
www.choicepoint.net

ChoicePoint is one of the nation's largest and most comprehensive sources providing public records information to businesses and government. Geared toward large clients, it tries to guarantee that its information will be used for legitimate business purposes. Don't use this one to find your old boyfriend.

PeopleData
www.peopledata.com

PeopleData searches through public records for the name you supply. In return for fees ranging from $10 to $60, you can find addresses, phone numbers, and background check information on anyone. You can even see a satellite photo of the person's house, if available.

Finding the Famous

"I never forget a face." Recent studies have shown that human brains devote specific single neurons to remembering each face we see (R. Quinn Quiroga, L. Reddy, G. Kreiman, C. Koch, & I. Fried. "Invariant Visual Representation by Single Neurons in the Human Brain." *Nature*, vol. 435, June 23, 2005, pp. 1102–1107). After all, our ancestors recognized members of their own small tribes by sight. It's no wonder that when we see celebrities on television over and over, our brains come to believe that we know those people. Maybe that is why we are so interested in the details of the lives of public figures and celebrities. Our brains consider them family!

The Internet Movie Database (IMDb)
www.imdb.com

Use this incredibly detailed and easy-to-use site to get the scoop on your favorite movie stars: biography, filmography, everything. I found out that Kevin Spacey is exactly one month younger than I am and that I probably competed against him in high school drama festivals, oh, some 30 years ago. Needless to say, he won.

Biography.com
www.biography.com

A&E Television Network brings you this searchable online database of articles about more than 25,000 of the greatest lives, past and present. Search by name or birth date. Click through to the *Biography* magazine pages that feature highlights of some issues, "Who Am I?" guessing games, and a "Where Are They Now?" archive. Did you know that Mr. T survived a 1995 bout with cancer and now spends his time visiting sick children? I pity the fool who doesn't visit this site!

Who2?
www.who2.com

The cabbie asks, "Where to?" Fritz Holznagel and his staff ask the question, "Who2?" Find information about famous folk fast with the Who2? search box, or use the name browse feature. Who2?

also features articles called "loops," linking celebrities that have something in common. Read the one about dead celebrities who are said to walk the earth as ghosts.

Chiefs of State and Cabinet Members of Foreign Governments
www.odci.gov/cia/publications/chiefs/index.html

Who is the president of Zambia again? Trust the CIA, which maintains this page, to keep you up-to-date on the heads of state.

Who's Behind that Web Page?

A quality Web page always offers a hyperlink to its author. This allows the user to evaluate the authority behind the information on that page and also provides a way to contact the author with questions or comments. But not every Web page is a good one. Unscrupulous dealers may very well put up pages lacking contact information. Is there a way to find out who is responsible for a particular Web site?

Yes, through the Internet Corporation for Assigned Names and Numbers, or ICANN (www.icann.org). ICANN is the nongovernmental organization to which the U.S. Department of Commerce transferred the responsibility for regulating IP address numbers and domain names on the Internet. ICANN is also responsible for managing who "owns the dot"; that is, it oversees the Internet root server system.

What does that mean in English? All Internet access points have IP (Internet protocol) addresses, such as 199.245.81.67, the IP address of the American Library Association Web site. But who can remember that long string of numbers? So ICANN accredits companies such as Network Solutions, Inc. (www.networksolutions.com) to act as registrars. These registrars are authorized to assign "domain names" to IP address numbers, resulting in the familiar "dot-com," "dot-edu," and "dot-org" URLs. For example, the domain name translation of the American Library Association IP address is www.ala.org.

Just to let you know, there are now new endings available for domain names in addition to the current "dot-com," "dot-net," etc., and country codes such as ".jp" (for Japan) and ".ie" (for Ireland). These new domain name endings include ".biz," ".info," and ".us."

To discover the name and address of an individual who registered a domain name, visit the registrar's home page and search its "WHOIS" database. This will reveal the contact information for the purchaser of that domain name. It will also provide you with a corresponding IP address for the domain.

InterNIC
www.internic.net/index.html

InterNIC is the service of ICANN that registers the companies that act as domain name registrars. Search here to find a company that can register a domain name for you, or help you find the contact information behind a mysterious one.

Better-Whois.com
www.betterwhois.com

For the first time, many different domain registrars are granting domain names. Each of these domain registrars now keeps their own WHOIS database, which doesn't include domains registered by competing registrars. This domain name registration search engine finds the appropriate registrar for the URL you seek, then queries that registrar's database for the correct information.

DNS Stuff
www.dnsstuff.com

R. Scott Perry has compiled this page of powerful tests to discover who is "paying the rent" for any Web page. Search by domain name or IP address. Use the "geolocation" tool to pinpoint the city and country of Web sites and e-mail addresses. Spammers and hackers have trouble disguising their identity from the worldwide reach of DNS Stuff.

Protecting Your Privacy

"Not everyone wants to be found," notes Carole A. Lane, author of *Naked in Cyberspace* (CyberAge Books, 2nd edition, 2002, ISBN 0910965501). Some of the reunions she has facilitated using online databases have been less than joyous. "(These reunions) may not be everything that was imagined all those years."

What can you do if *you* do not want to be found? Well, the free telephone searches do not pick up unlisted phone numbers, but if you own property, you will be listed in public records. Not only that, but commercial sites plant cookies and collect all kinds of demographic information on you in exchange for access to their "free" information.

Even your browser reveals information as you surf. This Privacy Threat Test (www.anonymizer.com/privacytest) tells you what your browser is revealing about you as you weave your way around the Web.

Not to worry. There are free tools available on the Web that will conceal your identity as you click around cyberspace. These applications are called "Jondos," short for John Doe, the pseudonym used to conceal identities in court cases. One software suite of such tools is called the Anonymizer (www.anonymizer.com), which is designed to let users surf and send e-mail in a way that makes it nearly impossible to trace. Another Web site called the Cloak (www.the-cloak.com) allows users to visit Web sites anonymously for free.

For more information on protecting your privacy in cyberspace, visit the Web site of the Electronic Privacy Information Center (www.epic.org).

Come Out, Come Out, Wherever You Are!

If you don't find the folks you seek through the services I have described here, then they probably don't want to be found. Also, you always have to question the completeness or comprehensiveness of these online databases. The information in them is only as good and reliable as the sources keying in the data. The data you want may be missing; the data you get may be inaccurate or outdated. Finding people using the Internet is still a matter of luck. It's just that your chances are much better than they used to be.

By the way, my grandmother, Orpha Esta, sprang suddenly into three dimensions for me when I found her death certificate listed in an Ohio Historical Society archive (www.ohiohistory.org/dindex) using Search System's public records search engine

Figure 2.3   I found Grandma on the Ohio Death Certificate Index.

(www.searchsystems.net). Orpha E. Brandenburg died on December 24, 1932, in Adams County, Ohio. Well, Grandma, all I can say is I hope that the fudge was worth it.

Good luck using the Web not only to fulfill your patrons' information needs, but their desire for human connection and community, too!

Chapter 3

News on the Net

After a hard day on the reference desk, I trudge tiredly through the back door, pour myself a glass of chardonnay, pluck up the remote, and thunk myself down on the couch to enjoy a little relaxation and catch up on the day's events. Turning on my TV, I see car wrecks, crime, conflict, and catastrophes, the "four C's" that form the staples of local newscasts. Look! Graphic photos! Look! Horrendous acts of violence! And that's just the local news.

News is gossip, really. We humans love to know what is happening, to hear the scoop, to be in the loop. Yet watching the local news on TV is like getting an earful from your mother about all the hateful things done by the children of the women in her bridge group. It's not only nasty, it's a waste of time. If I had more time, I'd read the newspaper, which I would then have to haul out to the recycling bin, heave to the top of the pile, and drag a whole stack out to the curb once a week for trash pickup. It makes me tired just thinking about it.

So, for decades now, I've gotten most of my news from the radio. This method, although time-efficient (if you listen as you get ready for work), still has its drawbacks. For instance, until he became terminally ill and began receiving career-spanning accolades, I had no idea that the late tennis great Arthur Ashe was African-American. Nobody on the radio ever mentioned it.

Fortunately for me, the World Wide Web was invented, and I finally had pictures to go with the stories I heard. Wow! Those panoramas from Mars were really cool! And look at the views from the Hubble! Now, that's gossip worth hearing *and* seeing.

Providing new and changing information is one of the things that the Web does best. In recent years, there have been tremendous advances in delivering breaking news stories from around the world via the Internet. Indeed, one of the great joys of being an information professional is being able to sneak a peak at the CNN site (www.cnn.com) several times a day and justify it as research. ("Hey, I have to keep up.")

I don't bring my computer on vacation though, and that sometimes leaves me feeling disoriented when I return. How dare big things happen while I'm gone. Again, it's the Web to the rescue. I can look back over the previous couple of weeks to recreate the news I've missed, maybe even specific radio and TV news broadcasts.

Maybe I take my news access too personally. But I am not alone. Our patrons and clients value the news, too, and not just for entertainment reasons. Businesses track news for competitive intelligence, investors monitor the value of their stocks, and folks with illnesses follow news of medical advances. Knowing what is happening in the world can make a huge difference in our patrons' quality of life and the success of their enterprises.

Web News Metaportals

When our patrons want an instant overview of the news scene, the news portals are a good place to start. Here are some sites that pull together major news feeds into one convenient place.

Yahoo! News
http://news.yahoo.com

Yahoo! serves up stories from 7,000 global news sources including the Associated Press and Reuters. It also has links to ABC News and its multimedia files. Yahoo! News is also a great search engine for recent news.

Google News
http://news.google.com

Is there anything that Google doesn't do? Visit this page to search and browse 4,500 news sources updated continuously by an automated news aggregator. Interestingly, much of the information comes from international feeds such as the Xinhua News Agency (www.xinhuanet.com or, in English, www.chinaview.cn) from the People's Republic of China. Search for recent news stories here, too.

NewsNow
www.newsnow.co.uk

How about some breaking news with a British flair? NewsNow offers "quality news headlines updated every five minutes, every day." Choose subject categories that you would like to study, such as business, information technology, or regional conflicts. Or jump directly to sports news of your favorite "football" (i.e., British soccer) team.

NewsHub: Headline News Every Fifteen Minutes
www.newshub.com

NewsHub, now owned by TuCows, currently makes more than 90 sources available in nine major categories, headlines updated every 15 minutes.

NewsIsFree
www.newsisfree.com

Visit Swiss-based NewsIsFree for top headlines from around the world. NewsIsFree also offers a customizable news feeder service for a fee.

Cyber Paperboy
www.cyberpaperboy.com

He's an auto mechanic! He's an Internet mogul! He's Cyber Paperboy! David Akerley, owner of D.J.'s Brake and Strut in Clawson, Michigan, washes the grease off his hands several times a day, rushes to the computer in the corner of his garage, scans the headlines on the wire services, and posts them, often faster than you can hear about them on your local station. "I'm not really a journalist," Akerley demurs. "I'm just like a regular paperboy." A paperboy who regularly scans and serves up newswire headlines before the major media outlets do.

Breaking News

Here are some major news outlets where folks can turn for a quick rundown of big events.

CNN.com
www.cnn.com

This is great first stop for up-to-the-minute headline news. You can get the latest in politics, business, sports, space, health, books, and travel. I use it to keep up-to-date on the latest breakthroughs in medicine. Also, the site allows you to search both its print and media archives for the past several years. They also offer video for a fee.

Reuters.com
http://today.reuters.com/news/default.aspx

Since 1851, Reuters, the British-based company founded by German émigré Paul Julius Reuter, has transmitted stock market information and other news around the world as fast as technology would allow. Get the latest today on its Web page or subscribe to its RSS feed. (More about this later in the chapter.)

BBC News
http://news.bbc.co.uk

The news division of the British Broadcasting Service (BBC) is one of the most sophisticated in the world. It delivers the pulse of the planet in many languages and formats. Get your worldview on this Web page, or have it delivered to your cell phone or news aggregator.

USA TODAY National and International News
www.usatoday.com/news/front.htm

It's fast and it's graphical, just like its print counterpart. Many sections feature columns and applications that add value to the basic headlines. For instance, the Travel section (www.usatoday.com/travel/front.htm) offers a flight tracker and an up-to-date "Control Center" that shows delayed flights across the United States.

FOXNews.com
www.foxnews.com

Murdoch-owned FOXNews skews to the masculine and conservative. If you share this bias, you will love this site. Health stories? Nah, too sissy. Science and technology? For geeks only. But there is plenty of sports news here, along with financial reports, entertainment features, and opinion. As they say on Fox, "You decide."

Streaming News

Think about broadcast media: television and radio. Before the Web, those transmissions occurred in real time. There were no archives. If you missed it, you missed it. Today, you can pull down these broadcasts over the Internet and replay them on your computer. It's amazing!

To get the full story off these sites, you will need plug-ins and helper applications, such as Apple's QuickTime and QuickTime VR (www.apple.com/quicktime), RealNetwork's RealPlayer (www.real.com), Windows Media Player (www.microsoft.com/windows/windowsmedia/default.aspx), or Macro-media's Shockwave (www.macromedia.com/downloads). Warning: Don't play this stuff too loud in your cubicle or in the Reference Room.

MSNBC
www.msnbc.msn.com

This is the only site that offers free video feed from recent news stories. Although the multimedia features of this news site are terrific, they can be tough for old computers and dial-up connections. Look here also for stories from *Newsweek* magazine.

The FeedRoom
www.thefeedroom.com

The FeedRoom is an independent online video broadcaster. View recent video news clips here for free (in return for watching a commercial, of course). Material is categorized by "channels," that is, subjects.

NPR.org
www.npr.org

National Public Radio (NPR) was born when Congress passed the Public Broadcasting Act in 1967. I haven't been listening to it quite that long, but it has been my primary source of news since college. Because NPR is a radio network, the programming on its Web site is primarily available through streaming audio.

The Online NewsHour
www.pbs.org/newshour/newshour_index.html

Listen to Jim Lehrer and the gang hash over the week's news in RealAudio. Some featured segments also appear in an online transcribed format.

Blogs

Now here's a thing that we have all heard about but may not necessarily have had much truck with. The word "blog" is short for "Web log." A blog is a Web site that does the cleaning for you, so you don't personally have to redo the HTML every time you want to add something new. This is especially useful if you want to post information frequently, but don't want the responsibility of taking off the old stuff.

This makes a blog the perfect format for posting news. At our library, we set up a blog at Blogger.com (www.blogger.com) to serve as our "What's New?" page (http://sanmarinopl.blogspot.com). To post new information, all I have to do is to cut and paste the text of our press releases onto the site's intuitive editing page. Old stuff is automatically shifted to an archive, still just one click away. But the information on the main page is fresh.

Very cool. And very often, the service is free (well, in the case of Blogger, the price is a small banner of advertising across the top of the site). So, many people have begun to post their thoughts on the Web using these blog services.

Blogs are free speech taken to its logical conclusion. As a result, most are worthless as a source of verifiable news. Still, a few blogs have gained a reputation of reliability, at least as the voice of a particular point of view. Some blogs have been picked up or sponsored by major news suppliers to serve as unedited color added to straight news reporting. An example is The Note, a morning news summary about politics from ABC News.com (http://abcnews.go. com/sections/politics/TheNote/TheNote.html). Correspondents may post from all over the world, right where news is happening. Sometimes bloggers break stories before the news outlets do.

How do we find blogs to read? Fortunately, directories exist to point the way. Also, many blogs feature a "blogroll," that is, a list of links to other blogs that the author prefers. Beware: You could spend your entire *life* reading these things.

Yahoo! Directory Weblogs
http://dir.yahoo.com/Computers_and_Internet/Internet/ World_Wide_Web/Weblogs

This time our old buddy Yahoo! offers a classified, handchosen directory of blogs. What's your pleasure? Law? Entertainment gossip? How about politics in any flavor that you prefer? Come here to find news with attitude.

FaganFinder: Blogs and RSS Search Engines
www.faganfinder.com/blogs

Here's a metasearch engine of search engines for blogs and RSS feeds. It's all laid out on one page and has a very clear interface. This is a great place to go blog shopping.

BlogStreet

www.blogstreet.com

BlogStreet offers a searchable database of blogs. Find blogs listed by popularity, subject, and even author. This site also features a blog directory listed by subject.

Technorati

www.technorati.com

What's the buzz in the blogosphere? Technorati monitors more than 3 million blogs in real time so you can discover the conversations happening now. View the "NewsTalk," politics, or book talk sections as they monitor the chatter.

Choose Your News: News Aggregator Sites

Now that you are addicted to reading blogs, you might find it inconvenient to visit each site that you like every day. This is not a problem anymore! You just need to sign up on a news aggregator, a.k.a. news-reader site. These sites can pick up the RSS feeds of your favorite blogs or news outlets and bring them all to one place for your perusal.

"What is RSS?" you ask. Karen Schneider, the "Free Range Librarian" (http://freerangelibrarian.com) and editor of the Librarians' Index to the Internet (http://lii.org), explains that the acronym RSS means various things, but her favorite definition is "Really Simple Syndication" (http://lii.org/search/file/liirss). When a blogger sets up an RSS feed, the text on the blog is converted into a format that a news aggregator can understand. The aggregator can pick up the RSS feed and display headlines and brief abstracts. Users can click on interesting headlines to get the whole story.

Another great thing about news aggregator services is that they can usually pull in the daily or weekly information bulletins or headlines that you would normally send via your e-mail. All too often the newsletters I've signed up to receive remain unread in my inbox. I filter them off into their own rarely viewed folder or dump them with the rest of the digital trash. How much better it is to have that stuff sent to a single Web site instead of my work mail.

Many news aggregators are programs that bring news down to your computer desktop. The following Web-based applications will keep the news off your computer and up on the Internet, making it accessible from anywhere you access the Web. Like blogs, news readers clean up after themselves automatically, showing only the latest news.

Bloglines
www.bloglines.com

This free Web-based news aggregator is easy to use. Sign up to pull in the information from your favorite blogs and news resources, including the *New York Times*. If you find an article that you want to keep, you can "clip it," that is, store it on-site to read it again later or send it to others. Bloglines offers space to users to set up their own blogs, too.

My Yahoo!: RSS Headlines
http://my.yahoo.com

You can use Yahoo! for e-mail, your calendar, and so many other things. Now use it as a news aggregator, too. Sign up for up to 50 feeds. Yahoo! suggests a few popular ones, such as Slashdot or the *New York Times* front page. Alternately, you can paste in a URL for any RSS feed that you like.

Fastbuzz News
www.fastbuzz.com

Register to use this free online news aggregator.

Rocket RSS Reader
http://reader.rocketinfo.com/desktop

This free Web-based RSS aggregator comes from Toronto.

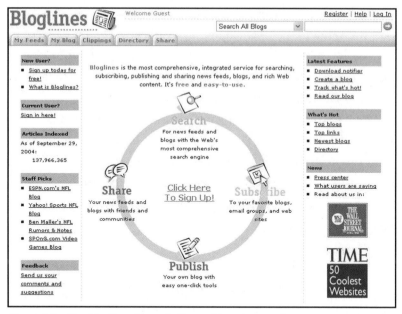

Figure 3.1   Use Bloglines to read all your blogs in one place.

Desktop News Readers

Most news aggregators are "clients" or programs that users download and use on a single computer. These programs still have the advantage that they don't hang on to old content unless you request it. Just read all the headlines as they appear, read the articles that please you, then let them disappear as more news comes down.

AmphetaDesk
www.disobey.com/amphetadesk/index.html

"AmphetaDesk is a free, cross platform, open-sourced, syndicated news aggregator—it obediently sits on your desktop, downloads the latest news that interests you, and displays them in a quick and easy-to-use (and customizable!) Web page." It works on Linux, Macintosh, and most versions of Windows.

NewzCrawler
www.newzcrawler.com

Another popular news-reader program is NewzCrawler. This one costs $25, but it allows customizable views of the news. Formats include scrolling list, News Balloon, and News Ticker.

Net News Wire
http://ranchero.com/netnewswire

This news aggregator client from Ranchero Software works on Macintoshes. It will set you back $40, but it offers users a familiar three-paned interface similar to Apple Mail and Outlook Express.

Find RSS Feeds

Most news aggregator programs and Web-based readers offer lists of the most popular feeds and make it easy to subscribe to them. For more in-depth directories of syndicated information, look to these sites.

Feedsters
www.feedster.com

It looks like Google but searches only RSS feeds.

2RSS.com
www.2rss.com

This Toronto-based Web site offers RSS feeds and a place to read them online. It also offers free software that will allow users to turn their own content into RSS feeds, too.

Syndic8.com
www.syndic8.com

Washington state programmer Jeff Barr built and runs Syndic8, which is dedicated to finding and listing all RSS feeds as they appear. Site editor Bill Kearney works as an RSS "evangelist"; he encourages Web content providers everywhere to offer their information in RSS format.

News Search Engines

Been on vacation for a couple of weeks? Or maybe a story that has been unfolding for a few cycles has just now caught your attention. Don't despair. In addition to the searching capabilities of Yahoo! and Google news services, try these engines to retrieve those stories that zoomed by you.

Daypop
www.daypop.com

Use Daypop to search 59,000 of the best news sites and Web logs on the Net every day.

NewsTrove.com
www.newstrove.com

Here is a metasearch engine of news sites from around the Web. Just enter a keyword, and you're off!

Figure 3.2   Daypop is a search engine for new sites and Web logs.

Directories of Online Newspapers and Archives

Librarians know the importance of the ability to get your hands on the local story. *MCLS Reference Hotline*, the newsletter of a library consortium in the Los Angeles area, made that point clearly: "Sometimes, when there is a major news story, the best news coverage comes from the area closest to the scene of the news. For example, last fall we had to verify a story that a patron heard on the radio about a mother 'accidentally' killing her infant son in a microwave oven. It was covered in *USA Today*, giving the location as Lanexa, Virginia, 35 miles east of Richmond. A search in the *Washington Post* listed stories from September 24–29, 1999, which gave far more details than the original national story" (*MCLS Reference Hotline*, No. 214, March 1, 2000).

Remember when you had to go to the library and haul out several smudgy newspapers to get a multidimensional view of a local news story? Yes, that worked if the story was local. Forget the inside scoop on national or international happenings. We had to be content with whatever papers we could put our hands on.

The Web has changed all that. Rare is the print paper that doesn't have a Web counterpart. Even the weekly from the small town where I work is online (the *San Marino Tribune*, www.san marinotribune.com). Foreign papers and other news sources are there for the reading, too.

Are you worried about events in the Middle East? Perhaps you might want to read the news from a variety of viewpoints so you can form your own conclusions. Get the Western overview from the New York Times online (www.nytimes.com/pages/world/middleeast/index.html) or the BBC Online Middle East Page (http://news.bbc.co.uk/1/hi/world/middle_east/default.stm).

View the news from an Arab vantage point at Aljazeera.Net English (http://english.aljazeera.net/HomePage). Then sample a conservative Israeli take on events at the Jerusalem Post (www.jpost.com). Just a glance at these different resources makes it easy to see why that region is so turbulent.

The Web is also a great place for alternative and college papers, as well as those papers with strong political or ethnic points of view. Here are some ways to find them.

NewsLink
http://newslink.org

Eric Meyer of NewsLink Associates manages this comprehensive directory of links to media with corresponding Web pages. Come here to find links to more than 4,000 American newspapers and 2,000 from other parts of the world. U.S. and Canadian publications are cross-indexed by location and type. Magazine, radio, and television Web sites are listed here, too.

NewsDirectory.com: A Guide to English-Language Media Online
www.newsdirectory.com

Use NewsDirectory to find English-language newspapers and magazines from around the world. These 3,600 newspapers and more than 4,800 magazines all have print counterparts, so no e-zines here. This directory is searchable by region, subject, or area code.

Newspapers Online!
www.newspapers.com/index.htm

Madison, Wisconsin-based Newspapers Online! is a searchable database of links to media worldwide. No browsing here, so users must know the name of the publication they seek, or at least the city in which it is published. This type of search is most appropriate for local resources like newspapers or employment sites.

U.S. Newspaper Links: USNPL
www.usnpl.com

No fancy graphics here, just a cool directory of U.S. newspaper links listed alphabetically by state. This site's *raison d'etre* is to sell a national newspaper mailing list to public relations people. Still, it's nice that they make their database available to everyone on the Web.

Abyz News Links
www.abyznewslinks.com

Perhaps you come from another country and long for news from the homeland. Then this is the site for you. Find media outlets with a Web presence from all over the globe—in your native language. (Anybody here read Urdu?)

News Magazines

Why are today's stories considered news? What is the story behind the story? News magazines can flesh out a tale and offer interpretations on the meaning behind the headlines.

Slate
http://slate.com/Default.aspx

A partnership between MSNBC and Microsoft brings us Slate magazine online. Slate offers intelligent takes on the news of the day and the week. Read it on your computer or your PDA, have it delivered to you e-mail inbox, or pick it up on your news aggregator via RSS.

Salon.com
www.salon.com/index.html

This hip mag provides sharp left-leaning insights into today's events. Subscribe to the site for easy access or trade viewing ads in return for day passes.

The Note
http://abcnews.go.com/sections/politics/TheNote/TheNote.html

To keep up with political news as it happens, visit The Note from ABC News. It features reporters writing about what other journalists are saying and writing. If you love political news, sign up to get The Note delivered to your e-mail box every day.

U.S. News Online
www.usnews.com/usnews/news/home.htm

Dive deep into today's important issues with the online version of U.S. News and World Report. You will look so smart!

Arts & Letters Daily: Ideas, Criticism, and Debate
www.aldaily.com

Editor Dennis Dutton publishes from New Zealand, gathering tidbits from online newspapers, feeds, magazines, e-zines, and columnists. I have seen no other news portal that discusses, on its opening page, the centenary of John Ruskin's death next to an article about how animal abuse predicts violence in humans. This is heady stuff, brought to us by the *Chronicle of Higher Education*.

World Press Review Online
www.worldpress.org

Teri Schure founded this site in 1997 to foster the international exchange of information. The site offers links to newspapers from around the world. Also, it offers synthesized, English-language capsules of the news from outside the U.S.

Capitol Hill Blue
http://chblue.com

Capitol Hill Blue's "recovering newspapermen," led by Doug Thompson, produce a lively, irreverent political news site. Here are plenty of mordantly sassy articles all about politics, published continually. Think Ambrose "Bitter" Bierce. Capitol Hill Blue's motto? "Nobody's Life, Liberty, or Property is safe while Congress is in session."

News Evaluation

These sites offer news about the news, a kind of "metamedia" critique.

NewsWatch: Views on the News
www.newswatch.org

The Center for Media and Public Affairs maintains this page, designed to "watch the media watchdog on behalf of news consumers." The Center aims to hold journalists to professional standards of fairness and accuracy. This site is especially good for rooting out bias in political coverage.

FAIR: Fairness & Accuracy in Reporting
www.fair.org

FAIR has offered well-documented criticism of media bias and censorship since 1986. It scrutinizes media practices that marginalize public interest, minority, and dissenting viewpoints. As an anti-censorship organization, FAIR exposes important but neglected news stories and defends working journalists when they are muzzled.

The Media Channel
www.mediachannel.org

The Media Channel collects lively writing from around the world that tries to keep reporters honest. Sample headlines: "USA Networks Drop the Ball on Political Coverage" and from Sri Lanka, "Minister Defends Climate for Journalists."

Jim Romenesko's MediaNews
www.poynter.org/column.asp?id=45

Romenesko gives up the goods on the backstage happenings in media news.

News of the Past

Elementary school kids come into my library and ask for help with their "history reports" about the September 11 terrorist attacks. It's a good thing that disaster has a date associated with it, or I wouldn't remember exactly when it happened. Still, when I re-read news reports from the time, the horror floods back. When I think

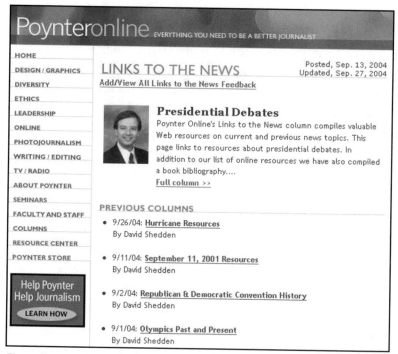

Figure 3.3   Get the background on the big stories of today and the recent past at Poynter Online's "Links to the News."

about newsworthy events in the past decades, I can recall exactly how they made me feel. Yet the precise dates of these occurrences frequently elude me. Fortunately, the following searchable databases of news from the past can help refresh my memory.

Slate: Today's Papers
http://slate.msn.com

The "Today's Papers" department offers clever précis of yesterday's major national newspapers to spare you the trouble of having to read them. Read it on site or have it beamed to your e-mail box, PDA, or RSS-based aggregator.

U.S. News Archives on the Web
www.ibiblio.org/slanews/internet/archives.html

Newspaper archives offer windows to the past. Volunteers from the Special Libraries Association keep those windows clear by maintaining a directory of links to U.S. newspapers with search-able archives on the Web. This directory provides the dates of the archive, along with the cost to retrieve the full-text articles. Newspaper listings are arranged by state.

Links to the News
http://poynteronline.org/column.asp?id=49

David Shedden writes the Poynter Institute Online's "Links to the News" column that compiles valuable Web resources on cur-rent and previous news topics going back to 1995. Remember the Oklahoma City bombing? You will after browsing these links.

All the News that Fits the Web

So you see, you can get your news any way you want it on the Web. Now, go on out there and find some good news for yourself and your patrons!

Chapter 4

Quality Reference Resources on the Web

I must confess to a bad habit. As gatekeeper to so much information for my community, I tend to get cocky. A client requests information such as, "I need some recipes for baking dog biscuits that contain no yeast or meat," and I immediately fire up my search engine and start clicking. Or "Tell me everything about Ninon de L'Enclos." Who? Or "Get me all the one-year Treasury bill rates back to 1985."

Whatever the request, I jump out onto the open Web and search and search. I hardly ever stop to think, "Whoa! There are people out there who do nothing but evaluate and annotate quality sites, then make lists available for my benefit. I don't have to wade through billions of hits then evaluate which sites are reliable all by myself. All that work has been done for me." Not only that, but these patient souls *maintain* their lists o' links so they don't get out of date, unlike any list that I would generate.

I refer to those handcrafted, meticulously manicured, and—how shall I put this?—*academically* oriented Web subject directories. Yes, Yahoo! has many links and does a pretty good job categorizing them, but that directory service's listings are not necessarily put together by librarians. Call me an elitist snob, but I just have to say it—nobody evaluates resources and organizes them better than we do. Nobody.

That being said, there are librarians out there, particularly academic librarians, who have taken it upon themselves to build intricate subject espaliers along academic lines. They prune away all but the clearest pathways to Web information. The result? An exquisite bonsai of information—authoritative, clean, yet detailed.

Browsing along a subject branch of that online bonsai is like wandering the stacks at a magnificent library. We may find the item that we wanted and then also discover others near it that suit our purposes even better. These carefully chosen, categorized collections foster research by serendipity, a method now recognized as legitimate, especially for humanities scholars.

What should we call these collections? They stand halfway between a portal and a vertical subject search engine with an academic twist. Shall we say they are "academic subject guides," "virtual reference collections," "a selective collection of topical guides"? "Topical guides" sounds like a skin ointment. For now, let us call these resources "meta-indexes," meaning collections of pointers to information organized by subject.

Whatever the name, these collections can satisfy both the subject browser and the information lounger. If clients need a piece of quality information quickly, these guides will point right to it. If we prefer a bit of background fill, we can click around through the categories, knowing that every site we find will be choice.

These quality subject portals definitely ease life at the reference desk. Following are some of the best.

Librarians' Index to the Internet
http://lii.org

If I pause long enough to actually *plan* a search before I reflexively type it into Google, I often turn first to the Librarians' Index to the Internet. Berkeley Public Librarian Carol Leita founded it in 1990 as a "Gopher" bookmark file. (Remember Gopher? It was a kind of hypertext way to telnet—before the Web.) Now run by librarian and "Internet Maven" Karen G. Schneider, the Librarians' Index to the Internet boasts links to more than 14,000 Internet resources in subject areas maintained by more than 100 librarian indexers. You need quality information from the Internet? You will

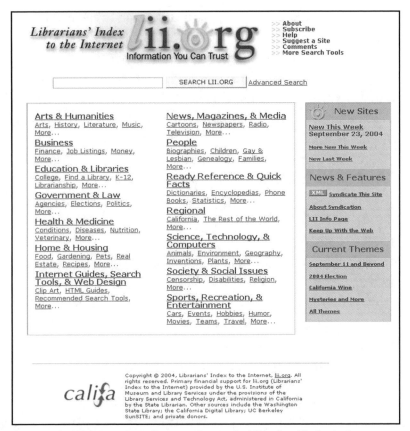

Figure 4.1   Librarians do well to turn first to the Librarians' Index to the Internet.

find it here, classified, annotated, and signed. The Librarians' Index to the Internet also features a current-awareness service, with new discoveries featured each week. You can choose to have this information e-mailed to you or pick up the RSS feed with your news aggregator.

The Internet Public Library (IPL)
www.ipl.org

In 1995, students in David Carter's graduate seminar at the School of Information and Library Studies at the University of Michigan thought up a way to answer reference questions over the

Internet. The gathered and annotated quality links serve as ready-reference resources for their project. That list of links, published on the open Web, has become the public face of the IPL. All links in its vast searchable collection have been carefully selected, cataloged, and described by a member of the IPL staff. Use the IPL "Pathfinders" (www.ipl.org/div/pf), that is, bibliographies of both Web and print resources, as strong starting points for doing research on particular topics. Patrons who do not wish to do a search themselves can submit an IPL "Ask a Question" form (www.ipl.org/div/askus). Don't expect an instant answer, though. The IPL staff and its network of volunteers receive so many queries that they have at least a three-day turnaround time.

Digital Librarian: A Librarian's Choice of the Best of the Web
www.digital-librarian.com

Margaret Vail Anderson, a librarian in Cortland, New York, has gathered a hefty selection of links filed under 90 categories. Most links sport a brief annotation.

Infomine: Scholarly Internet Resource Collections
http://infomine.ucr.edu

This compilation of academically valuable Web resources comes from the librarians at the University of California at Riverside. Sign up for their "New Resources Alert Service," which announces new additions by e-mail. Browse by subject or search their university-level collection by keyword, title, or author.

Pinakes, A Subject Launchpad
www.hw.ac.uk/libWWW/irn/pinakes/pinakes.html

Dave Bond and Roddy MacLeod of Heriot-Watt University in Edinburgh, Scotland, take their lead from the poet Callimachus, who compiled an index to the ancient Library of Alexandria. This catalog was called *The Pinakes*. "On a far smaller scale," Bond and MacLeod write, "these Web pages hope to provide a similar function for Internet resources, by linking to the major subject gateways." Especially British subject gateways. These include "Port," about maritime studies; "RUDI," which covers urban design; and "CAIN," which concerns "conflict studies," or, "the troubles" in Northern Ireland from 1968 to today.

Refdesk.com
www.refdesk.com/index.html

Bob Drudge, father of the Internet gossip Matt Drudge of the "Drudge Report," decided to "follow his bliss" in the spirit of Joseph Campbell. His bliss was to create this pretty darned comprehensive collection of Web links, "rationally indexed." Drudge writes, "Refdesk.com's database is on three levels: quick, studied, and deep. For thumbnail snapshots: 'FastFacts,' 'Quick Reference/ Research,' and 'My Facts Page.' For a more studied approach: 'My Virtual Newspaper' and 'My Search Engines.' For an in-depth exploration: 'My Virtual Encyclopedia' with 50 volumes of indexed subjects." Plus, the whole thing is searchable. Not bad for a guy who is really a psychologist. Did Mr. Drudge miss his true calling, in other words, librarianship?

BUBL LINK: Catalogue of Internet Resources
http://bubl.ac.uk/

From the Andersonian Library at the University of Strathclyde in Glasgow, Scotland, comes BUBL (originally, BUlletin Board for Libraries), a collection of selected Internet resources covering all academic subject areas. Naturally, it tends to slant toward British sites. Search in alphabetic or Dewey Decimal order.

Single Subject Portals

The collections I have just listed cover many disciplines. Yet many quality portals focus on narrow areas of study. Because of that focus, these portals often have more depth than general indexes and directories. If you have business in a particular subject area, give these portals a shot.

Humanities

Voice of the Shuttle
http://vos.ucsb.edu

Alan Liu is the larynx of the Voice of the Shuttle. A professor in the English Department at the University of California at Santa Barbara, Liu has compiled a tremendous list of resources in the humanities, those areas of study that may get short shrift in a Web culture geared toward technology and commerce.

Humbul Humanities Hub
www.humbul.ac.uk

This hub, originating from the "HUManities Communication BULletin Board" of the 1980s, is now part of the Resource Discovery Network (RDN) built by the British government to provide subject-based access to quality online resources. The Humbul Hub concentrates on language and literature, history, archaeology, religion, and philosophy. It is based within Oxford University's Humanities Computing Unit.

EServer.org
http://eserver.org

Iowa State University hosts EServer (formerly known as the English Server), a site that links to electronic texts in the arts and humanities. Their subject collections include art, architecture, drama, fiction, poetry, history, political theory, cultural studies, philosophy, women's studies, and music.

Social Sciences

ArchNet
http://archnet.asu.edu

ArchNet, from the Archeological Research Institute at Arizona State University, helps you find Internet resources in archaeology based on subject areas or region of study.

Social Science Information Gateway: SOSIG
http://sosig.ac.uk

Librarians and technologists from the Institute for Learning and Research Technology at the University of Bristol in the U.K. assembled this catalog, which they call "the Internet equivalent of an academic library, both from the users' point of view and from behind the scenes. Behind the scenes, librarians and technical staff use a combination of traditional library practices and database technology to create a quality collection which users can choose either to search or browse."

SocioSite
www2.fmg.uva.nl/sociosite/index.html

The University of Amsterdam hosts this "comprehensive listing of all sociology resources on the Internet." Come here to browse the "world wide scene of social sciences."

American Psychological Association
www.apa.org

This searchable gateway to all psychological issues includes access to professional information, psychology student info, and information on mental health topics designed for the public. Also access PsychCrawler (www.psychcrawler.com), a psychology-specific search engine.

Governments and Statistics

University of Michigan Documents Center
www.lib.umich.edu/govdocs/index.html

Grace York, the coordinator of the Documents Center at the University of Michigan Library, put together this central reference and referral point for government information, whether local, state, federal, foreign, or international. Its Web pages are a reference and instructional tool for those in government, political science, statistical data, and journalism.

FedStats: One-Stop Shopping for Federal Statistics
www.fedstats.gov

"More than seventy agencies in the U.S. federal government produce statistics of interest to the public. The Federal Interagency Council on Statistical Policy maintains this site to provide easy access to the full range of statistics and information produced by these agencies for public use."

Statistics Netherlands: CBS
www.cbs.nl/en

Statistics Netherlands, a Dutch government institution, offers links to official statistical resources from governments around the world.

Economics and Business

Hoover's Online
www.hoovers.com/free

When I need company information, I visit Hoover's first. Although much of the site is gated, guests can still get quite a bit of dirt on larger, public, mostly U.S.-based businesses, although the site lists some international enterprises, too. Free data includes company contact information, a link to the Web site, a few original paragraphs written about the company by Hoover's editorial staff, the names of several top executives, and the names of three top competitors. Key financial numbers are here, too.

Business.com
www.business.com

Search the "Business Internet" here. Mine specific company information or drill down through the directory to information for specific industries. Browse business news or look for job openings, too.

CEOExpress
www.ceoexpress.com/default.asp

CEO Patricia Pomerleau founded this site as an executive's interface to the Internet. "The site's peer editor recognizes that executives have precious little time to obtain all the information they require to conduct business. At the same time, much of the information that executives need is available on the Internet." CEOExpress claims to pare that information down to its most useful 20 percent by using expert human editors and "mind ergonomics." Much information here is free, but a premium level service requires a subscription.

BPubs.com: The Business Publications Search Engine
www.bpubs.com

BPubs is a search engine dedicated to finding free business-related publications and articles. Search by keyword or by browsing such categories as "Human Resources," "Finance and Accounting," and "Intellectual Property." Your results will include brief annotations of articles and links to the full text.

Inomics: The Internet Site for Economists
www.inomics.com/cgi/show

Inomics is an Internet portal especially tailored to the needs of economists. At this site you can find job openings for economists and conference announcements, as well as a search engine for economic information.

RFE: Resources for Economists on the Internet
http://rfe.org

Bill Goffe of the Department of Economics and International Business at the University of Southern Mississippi edits this collection, listing more than 1,000 Internet resources of interest to academic and practicing economists and those interested in economics.

Law

FindLaw
www.findlaw.com

This is the first-stop, premier, free law search engine on the Web. It features a legal subject index, access to cases and codes, information about law schools, law reviews, and legal associations and

Figure 4.2   Search for quality legal resources on FindLaw.com.

organizations. Are you a Supreme Court fan? FindLaw offers a comprehensive full-text searchable database of the Court's opinions back to 1893 (www.findlaw.com/casecode/supreme.html).

Legal Information Institute at Cornell University
www.law.cornell.edu

This is the research tool of choice to find the text of laws. Find state laws, federal laws, and laws from around the world. Here, too, you can find the full-text of all opinions from the Supreme Court back to 1990 plus the texts of more than 600 historic Supreme Court decisions (http://straylight.law.cornell.edu/supct/index.html).

The 'Lectric Law Library
www.lectlaw.com/index.html

Jeff Liebling's silly-yet-serious law site began as an early 1994 proposal to the Nevada University System for a nonprofit online legal information resource. Leibling mixes ASCII files of law information for professionals, students, and the general public with cheeky lawyer jokes. His idea is to spread legal knowledge in an online-friendly format while keeping visitors from getting bored. Lots of fun, but if you are really in trouble—skip this site and talk to a lawyer.

Science and Engineering

EurekAlert!: Your Global Gateway to Science, Medicine, and Technology News
www.eurekalert.org

The American Association for the Advancement of Science (AAAS), with technical support provided by Stanford University, produces this comprehensive Web site about the latest research advances in science, medicine, health, and technology. It also offers a selection of authoritative Web links divided into science subject categories.

National Science Digital Library (NSDL)
http://nsdl.org

The NSDL, funded by the National Science Foundation, is a digital library of "exemplary resource collections and services, organized in support of science education at all levels." Browse the alphabetical list of links, or use the graphical interpretation of their collection, clustered by subject.

iCivilEngineer
www.icivilengineer.com

Civil engineers, here is the portal for you. Read engineering news from around the Web and browse the directory of Web links by category. Scare yourself by reading the feature called "Failure Watch."

EEVL: Edinburgh Engineering Library
www.eevl.ac.uk

The EEVL Service serves as a gateway for the higher education and research communities to high-quality information resources in engineering. Subject experts select and maintain the catalog "to

Figure 4.3   Science, medicine, health, and technology news can be found at EurekAlert!

ensure that only current, high-quality or useful resources are included."

AgriSurf! The Farmers Search Engine
www.agrisurf.com

Under the motto, "More grain, less chaff," AgriSurf! offers a Yahoo!-like directory of everything agricultural, from "Aquacul-ture" to "Turf."

Medicine

MedWeb
www.medweb.emory.edu/MedWeb

The librarians at the Robert W. Woodruff Health Sciences Center Library at Emory University maintain this catalog of biomedical and health-related Web sites. MedWeb's primary audience is the academic and research community at Emory, so you can bet that these resources are top quality.

HealthWeb
http://healthweb.org/index.cfm

This directory of quality health resources stems from a collaborative effort between the Library of the Health Sciences at the University of Illinois at Chicago and the Committee on Institutional Cooperation's "HealthWeb" project. Click on a general ailment category to find links to all the major Web portals sites that address an issue.

Hardin MD: Medical Information + Pictures
www.lib.uiowa.edu/hardin/md

Eric Rumsey compiled this site for the Hardin Library for the Health Sciences at the University of Iowa. He writes, "As the name 'meta directory' implies, Hardin MD is a 'list of lists.'" Its purpose is to provide easy access to comprehensive resource lists in health-related subjects. Hardin MD also has links to medical pictures, so users can see what a brown recluse spider's bite looks like, for instance.

Guides Aplenty

When we reference desk professionals take advantage of vibrant, living subject guides crafted by our fellow librarians, we will appear as information gods to our clients, whoever they may be and whatever their area of interest.

Now ... if I can just remember to use them *first*.

Chapter 5

Internet Sites for Kids

I heard someone say that television viewing by children has decreased for the first time since television was invented. No, it's not because television is so bad, although it often is. It's because more and more kids have switched from TV to the Internet. Really! The World Wide Web is the first thing to come along in 50 years more compelling than the telly.

I wish the Web had been around when I was a kid. I wouldn't have watched all those reruns of *Mr. Ed*. Instead, I might have spent my childhood afternoons online, chatting with friends, shopping, or maybe even getting my homework done.

For kids who don't have Internet access at home or those who come to the library after school to wait for their parents to get off work, public Web access from the library has become a lifeline. It's not just an important study aid; it's also an enthralling babysitter. The Web just keeps getting bigger and better for youngsters, with more helpful and enjoyable sites popping up every day.

Although much of the Web is suitable for young eyes, problems can arise when we offer Internet access to both children and adults at the same public stations. A privacy screen doesn't help when one patron looks at an "adult" site, and the child who takes the next turn at the terminal pushes the "back" button or happens on an explicit pop-up. Whoa, Nelly! It makes me want to spray my keyboard with disinfectant just thinking about it.

This inconsonant mix of Internet users caused a problem a few years ago at the Los Angeles Public Library (www.lapl.org). L.A.P.L. is a gigantic, sprawling institution, with a huge Central hub and 71 branches. It is truly a "library of the people," serving recent immigrants from around the world and the homeless as well as the middle class.

When it became apparent that the Web use patterns of various populations at the L.A.P.L.'s public access Internet terminals were often "incompatible," as one might delicately put it, the Library realized it had a political time bomb on its hands. Its response was to construct a super-cool Web portal for children called "Kids' Path" (www.lapl.org/kidspath/index.html).

Figure 5.1   The Los Angeles Public Library offers a high-quality Web portal for children.

I talked about Kids' Path with Peter V. Persic, public relations director of the Los Angeles Public Library. He explained that this site offers links to librarian-chosen, age-appropriate Web pages that contain information that children ask for—ideas for science projects, for instance. Librarians have classified these links under subject categories.

In addition, Kids' Path features quick click-throughs to kid-friendly filtered search engines. What the library does *not* do, Persic emphasized, is filter the Internet access itself. "Any halfway-savvy child can maneuver around filters, anyway," he noted.

"We don't want parents to have a false sense of security," Persic continued. "They need to work with their children to teach them how to use the Internet effectively." Because kids often know more about technology than their elders do, the L.A.P.L. offers free computer classes for adults. These classes range from the most basic, for example, what is a mouse or how to use a keyboard, to more advanced instruction about how to conduct narrowly focused searches on the Web.

At least three dedicated Kids' Path computer terminals serve patrons in each Los Angeles Public Library branch, besides the bunch in the Central Library. Adults tend to avoid the terminals designated as Kids' Path, which effectively defuses the "back button" and pernicious pop-up problem. Children tend to follow the Kids' Path links or use the filtered search engines listed there. This strategy, for the most part, has successfully protected kids in the Los Angeles Public Library from the "dark side" of the Web—without the use of content blocking software.

It's a neat trick, separating incompatible Internet user populations by a kind of sleight of hand, a feat of "misdirection," as magicians might say. Bruce Chadwick of the Fort Worth Magicians Club (www.fortworthmagicclub.org/html/misdirection.html) explains the term: "Misdirection is really both focusing attention toward elements as much as away from other elements. Misdirection is the total effort to sway perception of an audience through the repel-divert-attraction process." In other words, keep your eye on Kids' Path. It is the magic that keeps the L.A.P.L. Web-using public—and their parents—happy.

The Los Angeles Public Library also offers a groovy portal aimed at teenagers. This site, called "Teen Web" (www.lapl.org/teenscape/index.html), matches the design of the cool study space for young adults at the Central Library. It offers homework help, links to help with life problems, and pages designed just for fun. It almost makes me wish I were 13 again. Okay, maybe not. Still, it's great.

Web Starting Points for Kids

These Web portals should satisfy kids, teens, parents, and librarians.

Yahooligans!
http://yahooligans.yahoo.com

Yahooligans! offers both a directory of educational and entertaining Web sites, plus a kid-friendly search engine. This is the most popular portal for kids outside of established library sites. It's safe, fun, cool, and entirely hand-picked.

KidsClick!
http://kidsclick.org

KidsClick! was created by a group of librarians at the Ramapo Catskill Library System. Like Kids' Path, it is assembled and maintained by librarians, but does not use filter software.

Internet Public Library Kidspace
www.ipl.org/div/kidspace

This is a terrific jumping-off point for all homework assignments.

ALA Cool Sites for Kids
www.ala.org/greatsites

Librarians have chosen more than 700 sites that they think will serve the interests of the little ones. The database is searchable by keyword, URL, and intended audience, in other words, appropriate for Pre-K youth, elementary school kids, middle-school students, and parents or caregivers.

IPL Teenspace
www.ipl.org/div/teen

Librarians have chosen these sites for teens to get help with homework and also to get advice about coping with life's stresses and strains. Get help with "Dating and Stuff" ("The Love Calculator" and "eCrush"), "Health" ("Go Ask Alice", etc.), and "Style" ("Nylon Magazine" and the "Bad Fads Museum").

Discovery Kids
http://kids.discovery.com
 The excellent science cable channel offers a wide variety of fascinating links for children and curious adults. Learn how to launch a fireball, become a mummy, or build your own roller coaster.

Search Engines for Kids

 Not only are these engines filtered, they also point to content specifically screened for children and teens.

Kids Tools for Searching the Internet
www.rcls.org/ksearch.htm
 Jerry Kunts of the Ramapo Catskill Library System in southeastern New York State put together this page of search input boxes from children's Web guides and filtered search services.

Ask Jeeves Kids
www.ajkids.com
 Yes, the inimitable Jeeves has been pondering what you are going to ask him. If he has been correct in his assumptions, you will get some good answers to your questions.

AOL@SCHOOL
http://school.aol.com
 America Online offers this search engine that links only to sites that are educational and safe for kids. AOL has some annotated links, too, to sites that are nothing but good clean fun. Search by subject and grade level.

Homework Help on the Web

 Where I work, in the affluent community of San Marino, California, homework isn't so much a learning tool for students as a competitive sport for their parents.

When the library doors open at 11 A.M., I am often confronted by svelte stay-at-home moms with master's degrees who have just received cell phone calls from their little ones. "My son has to do a report on mission San Luis Obispo." "What do you have on molds?" Or, "I need exactly 200 pages on Cabeza de Vaca."

What do these parents—or, even better, their kids—do about homework when the library is closed? Turn on the computer, of course, and jump onto the Internet. Many libraries offer access to high-quality gated resources to their patrons. Still, quite a bit of helpful, authoritative homework help exists out there on the open Web, if you know where to look. Here are a few of my favorites.

General Homework Sites

These specialized subject portals are dedicated to pointing homework-doers in the right direction.

Federal Resources for Educational Excellence (FREE)
www.ed.gov/free/index.html

More than 30 of the departments in the U.S. federal government have gotten together and put links to their educational resources on one site. The database is categorized into 10 subjects for browsing or use the search engine on the site to find exactly what you need. Your tax dollars at work!

Homework Help Sites for the King County Library System
www.kcls.org/hh/homework.cfm

Find the subject sites you need among 21 categories offered by the reference librarians of the King County Library system.

Information Please
www.infoplease.com

Information Please and its sister sites FactMonster (www.fact monster.com) and FunBrain (www.funbrain.com), for K–8 kids and teachers, all operate under the auspices of Pearson Education (www.pearsoned.com/about/index.htm), a large education publisher. Information Please is a fantastic general reference resource

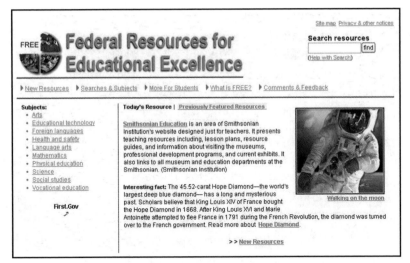

Figure 5.2   FREE is the U.S. government portal for kids.

featuring an authoritative encyclopedia, a dictionary, an almanac, and an atlas. FactMonster has access to all that information via a kid-friendly interface and a homework help center. Visit FunBrain for games with an educational edge, such as math-based tic-tac-toe or "Grammar Gorilla."

Pinchbeck's Homework Helper
http://school.discovery.com/homeworkhelp/bjpinchbeck

A former kid (now teenager) named B. J. Pinchbeck and his dad have identified over 700 homework helper sites and have arranged their collection by subject.

Columbia Encyclopedia, Sixth Edition
www.bartleby.com/65

Here's a free encyclopedia online. What could be more help than that?

Language Arts

Writing, and especially writing about reading, is one of the most difficult skills to teach. Practice is the only road to improvement. Here are some destinations to help you along the way.

Merriam-Webster Online
www.m-w.com

If you are going to write, you will need a dictionary and a thesaurus. Here they are together in one spot. Search a word in the dictionary and then search it in the thesaurus with just the click of an online button. This is a terrific tool.

A+ Research and Writing for High School and College Students
www.ipl.org/div/aplus

Kathryn L. Schwartz wrote this guide as a student in the Information and Library Studies program at the University of Michigan. It not only teaches writing but also steps for researching a paper using both print and electronic resources. Leave it to the Internet Public Library to mount such a useful resource.

Online Literary Criticism
www.ipl.org/div/litcrit

The Internet has never been kind to the humanities. Still, some hearty souls in academia care enough to mount literary criticism on the Web. If criticism is available free online, the Internet Public Library has found it and categorized it by date, by genre, or alphabetically by author name.

RhymeZone
www.rhymezone.com

Datamuse (www.datamuse.com) sponsors this excellent online rhyming dictionary and thesaurus. RhymeZone's results link to quotes from Shakespeare and other famous sources. Scroll farther down the home page to find quizzes, quotations, and the full text of important documents like the U.S. Constitution and the Bible.

Online Books Page
http://onlinebooks.library.upenn.edu

John Mark Ockerbloom, a digital library planner and researcher at the University of Pennsylvania, created and maintains the definitive, searchable directory to books freely readable over the Web. Because he only links to full text in the public domain, some of his entries pull up some rather obscure stuff. On the other hand, it can also find any copy of a classic you might need. Search by author, title, or Library of Congress subject heading. Find your Chekhov, Mark Twain, and Edith Wharton here.

Science

I remember my one and only science fair project. I glued a plastic drinking straw onto the skin of a balloon that was stretched across the mouth of an empty jelly jar. This was supposed to be a barometer. I don't recall that it worked at all, and needless to say, I did not win the science fair. But I kept that "barometer" in my room until its latex membrane crumbled.

Today, I would likely have a much more successful experience thanks to resources available on the Web. Most students these days are expected to prepare projects for an annual school science fair. These lucky kids have access to a wide variety of ideas, guidance, and up-to-date data on the Internet. The following sites will help youngsters with experiments and other science related reports.

Science Fair Central
http://school.discovery.com/sciencefaircentral

Visit the Discovery Channel's guide to science fair projects. Get guidance to the steps required in an experiment, get ideas, and search their links and suggested books for data.

Experiments and Science Fair from the Internet Public Library
www.ipl.org/div/kidspace/browse/mas6000

The Internet Public Library has assembled links to science fair sites from across the open Web.

Frank Potter's Science Gems
www.sciencegems.com

Physicist Frank Potter maintains this unmatched collection of science sites for students. He has amassed more than 14,000 science resources and sorted them by category, subcategory, and grade level. He has three separate collections of physical science sites, two earth science subcategories, two on life science, and one each on mathematics and engineering. Search the lot of them by keyword, too.

How Things Work
http://howthingswork.virginia.edu

Louis A. Bloomfield, professor of physics at the University of Virginia, answers questions from readers regarding the physics of everyday life. Users can search Bloomfield's archive of revealed wisdom by keyword, date, or subject. Find out why coffee seems warmer after you stir in cream, even though the cream is cold (transfer of energy). Discover the reason that paper towels absorb water (cellulose binds to water easily). And finally, uncover ways to make your coffee so hot in the microwave that the cup explodes. Science is fun! This site is great for high school students.

HowStuffWorks
www.howstuffworks.com

This subject-browsable or keyword-searchable database has articles aimed at kids from 9 to 11 years old. It is less formal and more accessible than the How Things Work site. I like the section on how computers work. I had a vague idea, but these articles explained the whole thing very clearly.

Weather.com Encyclopedia
www.weather.com/encyclopedia

Do you have an assignment where you have to report on a historically important storm? This is the resource for you. Check for historical descriptions of storms under "Hurricanes," "Tornadoes," "Winter Storms," and "Flooding."

NASA
www.nasa.gov

From the home page of the National Aeronautics and Space Administration (NASA), choose a variety of resources geared to various ages. There are student resources aimed at those in elementary school, middle school, high school, and college. NASA also offers information for educators, parents, and even games for preschoolers.

The Merck Manual Second Home Edition
www.merck.com/mmhe/index.html

When doctors and nurses get sick, they turn to the Merck Manual of Diagnosis and Therapy as their standard of diagnosis. But the medical terms in the regular Merck are often incomprehensible to the layperson. Students may prefer the Second Home Edition for the same great information translated into terms that all of us can understand. Completely searchable, this online publication lists the causes, symptoms, and prognosis of just about everything that can go wrong with you. It also covers mental conditions, pediatrics, and infectious disease.

MEDLINEplus Health Information
http://medlineplus.gov

The National Library of Medicine has assembled its resources onto one attractive portal designed for general health consumers. Students can visit this site to find information on conditions, diseases, drugs, and wellness. Also, they can use the handy medical dictionaries here to translate difficult medical terms.

Social Studies and History

Sociology is the study of how people behave (and have historically behaved) in groups. It also examines where people live and why. Trying to understand human behavior is enough to give anyone a headache. Here are some resources to cool your fevered brow.

HyperHistory Online
www.hyperhistory.com/online_n2/History_n2/a.html

HyperHistory covers 3,000 years of world history with an interactive combination of timelines, lifelines, and maps. Find and print historical maps here.

National Geographic Online
www.nationalgeographic.com

Use this site to play with a virtual solar system, make maps of anywhere on Earth, or learn to sail a boat interactively. Under "Homework Help," learn about history and culture, geography, animals, and nature. Teachers can join EdNet (http://ngsednet.org/index.cfm), an educational resource from National Geographic, for free.

FactFinder Kids' Corner!
http://factfinder.census.gov/home/en/kids/kids.html

The U.S. Census Bureau, in conjunction with Allison Druin from the Human-Computer Interaction Lab (HCIL) at the University of Maryland, serves up this page of kid-friendly facts from the 2000 Census. This is a great place to get the latest population and demographic information for those ubiquitous state reports.

ClassBrain's State Reports
www.classbrain.com/artstate/publish

If you have a state report due, visit here first. ClassBrain provides maps and links to state sites, and carries interesting local lore from each congressional district. Print handsome templates to give a polished look to your report.

Outline Maps
www.eduplace.com/ss/maps

The Houghton Mifflin Company offers quality outline maps of the United States, Europe, and the rest of the world free for homework use. Some maps appear in .pdf format and require the free Adobe Acrobat reader to see them.

Math

Yes, I *was* the only drama major in my college pre-med calculus class. But that was 20 years ago. I must confess, in the decades since, I have never once had the opportunity to calculate the rate of change of the rate of change. So, when a student asks me for help with his or her math homework, I am often stumped. I turn to these sites for help.

Math.com
www.math.com/index.aspx

Though a commercial destination, this site can nevertheless be a big help to those with math problems. Use this site to explore everything from addition to advanced calculus. A nice section here called "Everyday Math" can really bail out grown-up boneheads like me who still need a good half hour to remember how to calculate square footage for a home improvement project or how to convert recipe amounts from British to U.S. units.

Ask Dr. Math
http://mathforum.org/dr.math

Over the years, many people have written to the Math Forum at Drexel University in Philadelphia, Pennsylvania, with questions about their math homework. The Math Forum has collected these questions and answers in a searchable archive arranged by general grade level. Did they ever answer one of your questions? Feel free to submit your query to Dr. Math.

QuickMath
www.quickmath.com

Sometimes, you just want answers. Turn to QuickMath, developed by Australian Ben Langton. Type in an algebra or calculus problem and the MathScript server calculates results for you. This is a particularly nice site for lazy high school and college students.

Webmath from Discovery.com
http://school.discovery.com/homeworkhelp/webmath/

This site too invites you to type in your equations and get the answers. Just to check your work, of course.

Other Handy Tools

Biography.com
www.biography.com

Use this site to "search over 25,000 of the greatest lives, past and present." The site does not give out in-depth information, but at least it will give you a handle on the subject of your biography report.

FindArticles.com
www.findarticles.com

Need articles? Search this free archive of 5.5 million full-text articles dating back to 1998 from more than 900 magazines and journals.

MagPortal.com
http://magportal.com

MagPortal collects and classifies links to newsletters and magazines that offer current, interesting, yet free content on the Web.

Learn 2 Type
http://learn2type.com

No matter what, if you want to use the Web, you have to learn how to type. For those of us who didn't endure that excruciating typing class back in junior high school, this free service can help move us beyond the hunt-and-peck stage. Register for free and take the typing course for adults, or the Learn2 Type for Kids program. Learn 10-key here, too.

Free Touch Typing Program
www.senselang.com

Here is a simple browser-based typing tutor. Use the typing lessons on the site or paste in your own text for practice.

Child's Play

As much as we controlling librarian types hate to admit it, playing online games and other general goofing around on the Web is a legitimate path to computer mastery. If, in order to play *Donkey Kong*, I have to learn how to type, you can bet that I will do it, at least enough to play the game. On the other hand, many graphics-intensive games need mucho macho processing power and can hang up all but the newest computers. Also, these games can make a lot of noise and attract crowds. Additionally, the games monopolize public access terminals better used to help serious researchers find information they need. Still, it's a great way to get kids and teens into the library and onto electronic resources.

Playing is the *work* of children. Put your noses to the grindstone on these sites, kids!

Little Guys

PBS Kids
http://pbskids.org

PBS little kids, that is. Here, you will find tie-ins to *Teletubbies*, *Arthur*, *Barney*, and *Zoom*, which as I recall, was on TV when *I* was a child.

Nick, Jr.
www.nickjr.com

Play along with *Blue's Clues*, *Little Bill*, and *Dora the Explorer*. If you do not have children under the age of 5 … you have no idea what I'm talking about.

Sesame Workshop
www.sesameworkshop.org/sesamestreet

Sesame Street has been my favorite children's show since it first aired back in the 1960s. Originating from New York City, *Sesame Street* features some of the best writing and performing talents in our nation. It's Broadway for babies. Unfortunately, my son is now too old for it. But I can always sneak a peak at the Web site.

Elementary School Kids

Scholastic Inc.
www.scholastic.com/kids/home_flash.asp

Scholastic publishes most of the super-popular kids books available today: *Goosebumps, Captain Underpants,* and the star of stars, *Harry Potter.* The titles are basically responsible for a reading mania among children and teens. Play their games and order their books here.

MaMaMedia.com
www.mamamedia.com

Calling itself "The place for kids on the Net," MaMaMedia provides a space where kids can create Web site collections, design their own multimedia characters and stories, join computer clubs, and engage in many other interactive activities in a safe environment. All the activities are based on research done at Harvard University and the Massachusetts Institute of Technology on how kids learn best.

Kids' Castle
www.kidscastle.si.edu

The clever folks at the *Smithsonian Magazine* have come up with this attractive and fun site for kids. Use this site to play games, write messages on different topics, and read interesting articles written for the young set.

Headbone
www.headbone.com

"More than anything else, kids have a tremendous desire to connect and communicate with their peers. Headbone has pioneered the development of kid-oriented, safety-minded community and communications technologies on its site." Children between the ages of 8 and 14 can use this site for e-mail and safe, monitored chat, and to play games and win prizes.

Bonus.com
www.bonus.com

This graphics-intensive site from the WB Network offers plenty of gaming fun based on WB Kids programming.

Cartoon Network.com
www.cartoonnetwork.com

Come here to learn about your favorite cartoons, play games, and enter contests.

Funschool
www.funschool.com

Funschool offers more than 300 educational games designed for children between the ages of 3 and 11. These games follow established curriculum standards that can reinforce and supplement school classroom activities. A word of caution: This site is part of the Kaboose Network, an online marketing company. Users endure several ads before reaching the games. This same company runs Zeeks (www.zeeks.com), designed for young teens.

Teens

JavaGamePlay.com
www.javagameplay.com

Wow! Free arcade games online! It's all in Java, so you won't have to add plug-ins. What a time-waster, but what a lot of fun!

Zap2It
www.zap2it.com/index

If it's on a screen, it's in this 'zine. Get the latest gossip about the world of television, movies, and the Internet here, courtesy of Tribune Media Services.

ESPN.com
http://espn.go.com

"You can get all your sports and your stats—anything you want!" reports my colleague, a sports-fanatic librarian. This is the major portal for sports news and information.

Xanga
www.xanga.com

The teens at my library love to blog on this site. They run blog-rings to hold a kind of asynchronous conversation with all their friends.

Bolt
www.bolt.com

This is a portal for the coolest of the cool on the teen scene. Not only does Bolt offer voice and e-mail, but also "zap" instant messaging, chat, clubs, and what they call a "tagbook." Get your horoscopes and shopping sites here.

Protecting Kids

Do you remember that guy, Jack Hornbeck, who ran the child porno ring off the Los Angeles Public Library computers in the late 1990s? Three years and eight months he got for embodying the worst nightmares of every parent and librarian: using library computers to distribute pornography and arrange sexual liaisons with children.

"Although the vast majority (estimated at between 90 and 97 percent) of the Internet is terrific, a portion of it can be considered dangerous to children," writes Internet safety advocate Parry Aftab. "There are three kinds of dangers for children online ... information, child pornography, and online and off-line predators."

When it comes to offering Internet access to the public, it almost seems as though a librarian just can't win. Let's face it. If you filter, you violate the U.S. Constitution. Okay, so maybe your neighborhood is so conservative, they don't mind. Still, it's our job as information professionals to defend the right of adults to read or see whatever they choose.

On the other hand, there's some repulsive stuff out there, and plenty of lowdown characters clamoring to download images so disgusting that they could curdle milk—at taxpayer expense, of course. What's a librarian to do?

These sites offer advice and tips to answer that question. And they explore the issues involved in offering Web access to children.

ALA Safety Tips
www.ala.org/ala/pio/availablepiomat/safetytips.htm

The American Library Association brings you these safety tips for parents of children using the Internet. These common sense rules stress a parent's involvement with a child's computer use. Even if a child uses a filtered terminal, the ALA states emphatically, "We strongly recommend that you supervise your child's Internet use at home and at the library."

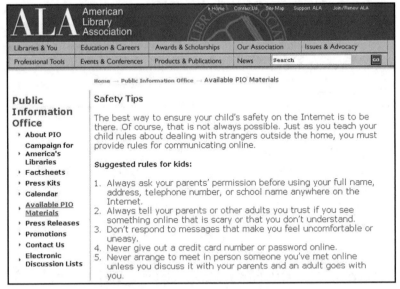

Figure 5.3   The American Library Association gives tips to parents about children's computer use.

Getting Started Step-by-Step
www.childrenspartnership.org/pub/pbpg98/partII98.html

The Children's Partnership offers parents clear explanations of the issues surrounding their children's Internet use. The site addresses within a historical perspective parents' understandable reluctance to have their children push ahead on something they do not understand themselves. A chart shows questions that parents have asked about new technology over the last 100 years. They show, for example, that in the 1890s parents asked themselves, "How can I afford a telephone at home?" In the 1920s, they asked, "Why do my children know more about radio than I do?" Fifty years later, "Are TV programs too violent?" And finally, now they ask, "Is being online safe and beneficial for my child?" Kinda makes you wonder what parents will have to worry about next.

CyberAngels.org: Internet 101
www.cyberangels.org/internet101.html

CyberAngels is an online safety, education, and help group run by volunteers. Visit their "Internet 101" page for tips on how to keep you and your kids safe out on the open Web.

SafeKids.com
www.safekids.com

Larry Magid, a broadcaster and syndicated columnist, runs this site as part of his "Online Safety Project" (OSP). Magid offers tips for kids and parents to help them avoid disagreeable Web sites and provides links to filtering software for use at home, as well as ISPs that offer filtered content.

From Soccer Mom to Super Internet Librarian Mom

The Yahooligans! Parent's Guide (http://yahooligans.yahoo. com/parents) asks, "Do the positives of allowing your child

Internet access outweigh the negatives?" It answers itself with a resounding, "Yes!"

"Allowing your child access to the Internet helps to ensure that they will be adept at finding, processing, and exchanging information—all valuable skills. It would be a shame to prevent your child from experiencing the educational and entertainment resources available via the Internet, especially when many of the problems that arise online can be easily addressed or prevented."

I couldn't have said it better myself.

So much exists out there now on the Web for kids that it might take all of a childhood and adolescence to go through it all. Young people could be entertained and enlightened for years without ever having to move from the computer chair. Now, if only we could get superfast Internet connections into the backs of our minivans for those long road trips. With wireless Internet access on the rise, that day may be just around the corner.

Chapter 6

Free Full-Text Resources

"A classic is a book nobody wants to read
and everybody wishes to have read."
– Mark Twain

I know that teachers do not really think first about their local public library when they assign a reading project to an entire grade level at their school. Where I work, we do carry at least six copies of *The Adventures of Huckleberry Finn*, and that is normally an excessive amount. But when 150 15-year-olds demand that book all at the same time, the atmosphere in the fiction section tends to get a little tense.

I have heard about devotees of "open source" coding: programmers working mostly in Linux who write computer code and share it with others for free. It occurred to me that there are people out there who do the same thing with literature. That is, they take the time to key in or scan page after page of works in the public domain then maintain them on the Web so we can all read them— without paying a cent. Could these resources help ease libraries' occasional literature shortages?

The Great Books Movement and the Internet

Collections of full-text books online often contain the "Great Books" of the Western canon, as described by the late University of Chicago president Robert Maynard Hutchins and his protégé, Mortimer J. Adler in the 1930s and '40s (www.greatbooks.org/typ/104.0.html). Considered by some to be "the original sources of our intellectual tradition" and "the seminal works that have shaped the world in which we live," these are the texts written by dead white guys that we were supposed to read in college—but perhaps never quite finished. Although some in academia now question the relevance of the "Great Books," many colleges still use Hutchins' list as the basis of their lower division humanities programs.

In any case, it's nice to know that these classics are so freely available out on the open Web, especially when you consider that the humanities generally get such short shrift in the online world. But who put them there? How did such an unlikely phenomenon get started?

The movement toward open source classics began in 1971 when student Michael Hart received a computer account with 100 million dollars worth of time in it at the Materials Research Lab at the University of Illinois. He asked himself, how could he repay this amazing gift of electronic access? As an answer, he typed in the *Declaration of Independence* and distributed it to everyone on his network—whether they wanted it or not. Hart's philosophy? Once a copy of a work has been entered into a computer, especially in a plain "vanilla" ASCII format, then everyone in the world can possess it.

Hart ceased the unsolicited distribution of his ASCII works and, instead, mounted them on the Internet where all who wanted them could find them. From this effort came Project Gutenberg, the "ur-site" of all full-text, public domain books on the Web.

Project Gutenberg
http://promo.net/pg/index.html

Michael Hart, along with volunteers, keys in mainly English-language literature that is unmistakably in the public domain in the U.S., that is, published before the mid-1920s. He breaks down his selections into three categories: "light literature," for example,

Alice in Wonderland; "heavy literature," for example, the *Koran* and the works of Shakespeare; and reference works such as *Roget's Thesaurus*. Find thousands of works here, free for the reading— and taking.

Handmade or Book Trade?

What is the difference, you may ask yourself, between Hart's labor of love and commercial e-book providers such as NetLibrary (www.netlibrary.com/Gateway.aspx), now a division of OCLC? The big divide is philosophy: Hart believes in access over profits, and NetLibrary wants to make money. NetLibrary sells access to new books and provides public domain offerings gratis. Their digital monographs have cataloging records at OCLC, which also stores copies of all the books. Also, the user interface at NetLibrary is very attractive, whereas the ASCII settings of Hart's books are purpose-fully plain. Yet, although NetLibrary allows guests to read public domain offerings online, visitors are not permitted to download or manipulate the texts. These privileges are reserved for patrons who have registered with the site through a library provider that has paid for a contract with NetLibrary.

Directories of Literary Electronic Text Archives

Given that freely available literary electronic text archives usu-ally contain only material in the public domain and that they don't bring much revenue to their makers, you can imagine that such collections tend to be eclectic at best; you might almost call them incomplete, haphazard, spotty. How can you tell where or whether the book you want to read exists online? By using one of these handy directories, of course!

The Online Books Page
http://onlinebooks.library.upenn.edu

John Mark Ockerbloom, a digital library planner and researcher at the University of Pennsylvania, created and maintains this definitive, searchable directory to books freely readable over the Web. Ockerbloom founded The Online Books Page in 1993, while a student at Carnegie Mellon University. In 1999 he moved it to its present location at Penn. Because he only links to full text in the public domain, some of his entries pull up rather obscure stuff. On the other hand, it can also find any copy of a classic you might need. Search by author, title, or Library of Congress subject heading. Find your Chekhov, Mark Twain, and Edith Wharton here.

UT Library Online: Electronic Books
www.lib.utexas.edu/books/etext.html

The General Libraries at the University of Texas at Austin is hot on electronic texts. In addition to providing a gateway to NetLibrary, the commercial e-text provider, this site also links to materials produced at the university and full-text resources on the Web.

Online Collections of Literary Electronic Text

So many of these collections of online books are the labor of love of a single person. Often, these collectors gather the raw text of books from Project Gutenberg, then reformat and classify works to their taste. Another approach is to mount new works that have not yet encountered a printer's press. Feel free to try them all.

Bartleby Library: Great Books Online
www.bartleby.com

What a great place to start looking for full English-language text resources in the public domain. Begun as a personal research experiment by Steven H. van Leeuwen in January 1993, this site allows the user to perform author, title, and subject searches for works of fiction, nonfiction, verse, and reference. Find everything here from *Gray's Anatomy* to works from the *Harvard Classics Shelf of Fiction.*

Electronic Text Center at the University of Virginia
http://etext.lib.virginia.edu

The University of Virginia has set itself a double mission: to digitize many classic tests not only in English, but also in other languages including Chinese, Korean, and Cherokee; and also to teach digitizing techniques to its community. Its fantastic subject collections include African-American poetry, Women Writers, and links from the Western European Specialists Section. Although many of its links are restricted to those affiliated with the university, quite a good selection is freely available for reading purposes to the general public. This is a world-class collection of e-texts.

Bibliomania
www.bibliomania.com

This U.K.-based source offers the classics in all their manifestations: novels, poetry, plays, and short stories. Bibliomania's pages are easily accessible by speech software, so that the visually impaired can have their Austen, Dickens, Shakespeare, and Twain read to them. Search by author and title, or by phrase appearing in the text of a document. Students can access study guides to classic texts.

Alex Catalogue of Electronic Texts
www.infomotions.com/alex

Librarian Eric Lease Morgan of Infomotions, Inc. has collected the ASCII editions of American and British literary texts, as well as works of Western philosophy, and put them on his server. From there, you can download them in PDF or compressed format. Browse for texts by author, title, or date.

EServer.org
http://eserver.org

Iowa State University hosts EServer, a site that links to electronic texts in the arts and humanities. Full-text books on EServer include the complete works of Edgar Allen Poe, the *Narrative of the Life of Frederick Douglass, American Slave,* and Sigmund Freud's *Interpretation of Dreams.* EServer, once known as the English Server, began at Carnegie Mellon University in 1990 under the direction of Geoffrey Sauer. In 2000, Sauer took his interactive, member-run, e-text cooperative to the English Department of Iowa State University (http://engl.iastate.edu/homepage.html), where he now teaches.

Oxford Text Archive
http://ota.ahds.ac.uk/menu/index.html

Founded in 1976 by Lou Burnard, this site collects, catalogs, and preserves high-quality electronic texts for research and teaching. The OTA currently distributes more than 2,500 resources in more than 25 different languages. Some are freely searchable and down-loadable over the Web; others require written permission.

Litrix Reading Room
www.litrix.com

Anchorage, Alaska-based mystery novelist Stan Jones collected his favorite ASCII texts (mostly from Project Gutenberg), converted them into a nice, clean HTML format, and placed them on his site. He divides his collection into several subject areas, including "Antiquities," "Ms. Austen & Co.," and "The North," that is, books about Alaska and environs. Brrr!

Blackmask Online: A Provider of Internet Literature
www.blackmask.com

David Moynihan has put his bachelor's degree in English to work by collecting almost 3,500 works of literature, especially tales of mystery and horror. These he has converted from plain ASCII into formats usable by Microsoft Reader, Acrobat, Rocket eBook, Palm Pilot, and Franklin's eBookman. He offers them to all of us gratis.

Luminarium
www.luminarium.org

Another thirtysomething scholar of English has crafted a fabulous full-text resource. Anniina Jokinen not only collects electronic versions of medieval, Renaissance, and 17th-century English literature resources, but also provides supplementary scholarly materials and a beautiful layout, complete with images from the manuscripts of the period.

Figure 6.1   Read medieval English texts amid glorious illustrations at the Luminarium.

Dime Novels and Penny Dreadfuls
www-sul.stanford.edu/depts/dp/pennies/home.html

The Stanford University Libraries have chosen nine of the best of their extensive collection of dime novels, which were the working-class recreational reading of choice in the late 19th century. Read for yourself the story of *Nick Carter, Detective: The Solution of a Remarkable Case* by "a celebrated author," or study *Adventures of Buffalo Bill from Boyhood to Manhood*, by Colonel Prentiss Ingraham. What fun! Great pictures, too.

Figure 6.2   The Dime Novels at Stanford University were just the thing for "reluctant readers" in the 19th century.

Documenting the American South: Library of Southern Literature

http://docsouth.unc.edu/southlit/texts.html

Would you like to read some Joel Chandler Harris or sample some Kate Chopin? Visit this site, officially known as "A Digitized

Library of Southern Literature, Beginnings to 1920." This collection is based on a list of the 100 most important works of Southern literature prepared by the late Robert Bain, professor of English at the University of North Carolina at Chapel Hill. Funded initially by a Chancellor's grant, its ongoing development is sponsored by the Academic Affairs Library at the University.

The Internet Classics Archive
http://classics.mit.edu

Daniel C. Stevenson of Web Atomics has mounted 441 mainly Greco-Roman works, along with some classics originally written in Chinese and Persian, all in English translation. Browse to find your favorites and to discover little-known gems.

Victorian Women Writers Project
www.indiana.edu/~letrs/vwwp

Perry Willett of Indiana University acts as the general editor of this highly accurate transcription of the works of more than 40 British women writers of the late 19th century.

Short Stories at East of the Web
www.short-stories.co.uk

East of the Web brings us the complete texts of "classic" (read "old") short stories, as well as new and otherwise unpublished ones. We can view them in HTML format or convert them to read on our Palm Pilots.

Individual Authors

Scholars have built entire sites around the greatest authors. Here, scholars have not only gathered the digital texts, but fabulous supporting materials, too. Visit these sites to get in-depth analysis of these writers, including literary criticism, Webliographies, and links to images related to authors and their works.

The Complete Works of William Shakespeare
www-tech.mit.edu/Shakespeare

This resource was created by Jeremy Hylton, a graduate of the Massachusetts Institute of Technology. The oldest school paper at MIT, the *Tech* (www-tech.mit.edu), maintains this database.

John Milton Reading Room
www.dartmouth.edu/~milton

Associate professor of English at Dartmouth College Thomas Luxon and his students have assembled the Milton Reading Room. It offers "most of Milton's major poetry in English and some of his prose. Many, but not all of the works presented here have been fully annotated." Check out the links to selected criticism.

Lewis Carroll Home Page
www.lewiscarroll.org/carroll.html

Joel M. Birenbaum edits this site, which offers an illustrated, hypertext version of *Alice's Adventures in Wonderland*, *Through the Looking Glass*, and *The Hunting of the Snark*.

Nathaniel Hawthorne (1804–1864) Home Page
www.eldritchpress.org/nh/hawthorne.html

Eric Eldred and Eldritch Press offer this searchable site containing just about anything you'd ever want to know about Hawthorne, including many of his works in full text.

The Cervantes Project
www.csdl.tamu.edu/cervantes/english

Eduardo Urbina is the editor of the Cervantes Project, housed at Texas A&M University. Find the full text of Cervantes's works here in both Spanish and English. Urbina provides a lot of fabulous supporting materials, too, including a biography of the author and a "Don Quixote Dictionary."

Poetry

The Web is a terrific medium for poetry. Poems are just the right length to read online. The Web also offers poets a way to distribute their work to reach verse lovers around the world. Use these sites to find great old poems, and new ones, too.

Sonnet Central
www.sonnets.org

Eric Blomquist loves a sonnet, and so he made this page all about them. Search for a favorite or write your own and post it.

American Verse Project
www.hti.umich.edu/a/amverse

The Humanities Text Initiative and the University of Michigan Press have assembled this searchable archive of American poetry from the 18th, 19th, and early 20th centuries.

The Poetry Archives
www.emule.com/poetry

Search almost 4,000 classic poems from nearly 150 authors.

Poets' Corner
www.theotherpages.org/poems

Bob Blair, Jon Lachelt, Nelson Miller, and Steve Spanoudis have archived over 6,700 English-language, copyright-free poems on their site. "Our goal," they report, "is to create the largest, most diverse, and most user-friendly public library of poetic works ever assembled." Search the archive by title or poet name.

British Women Romantic Poets, 1789–1832
http://digital.lib.ucdavis.edu/projects/bwrp

Nancy Kushigian, of the Shields Library of the Department of Humanities and Social Sciences at the University of California at Davis, has overseen the digitization of the Library's Kohler Collection. This collection consists of the work of more than 30 female British poets, from the Romantic era. Browse this SGML and HTML collection by author or by a simple keyword search.

Concordances

In the print world, a concordance is an alphabetical directory of words appearing in a text. Concordances are useful in locating the passage you seek in a classical work, for instance. They can also be used to analyze the word use patterns of authors such as Shakespeare. These patterns can then be applied to establish the provenance of disputed works. A hypertext concordance is even more useful, allowing the user to jump to word instances with a mere click of the mouse, and turning a research tool into a quotation dictionary.

Concordances have more functionality than plain vanilla full-text search engines that merely find words and might count their occurrences. Use a concordance to see where two words might appear within proximity of each other, or type a set of letters to find all word completions in a text; for example, typing "contain" gets "contains" and "container." You can have all sorts of word fun with a hypertext concordance!

The Web Concordances
www.dundee.ac.uk/english/wics/newwics.htm

The English Department at the University of Dundee, Scotland, has concocted concordances to certain poems of Percy Bysshe Shelley, and to certain poems of Samuel Taylor Coleridge, John Keats, William Blake, William Wordsworth, and Gerard Manley Hopkins.

Literature in Languages Other than English

Haven't I been just so Anglo-centric? Don't they call it the *World Wide Web*? Plenty of literature available online is not in English. Here is a sampling of some of the resources.

Perseus Digital Library
www.perseus.tufts.edu

Talk about your resources in the public domain! Perseus, from the Department of Classics at Tufts University, features online resources of the ancient world. Find everything old here, from Egyptian Papyri to materials from the Renaissance. You will need to download Greek fonts to see some of this material (see www.perseus.tufts.edu/Help/fonthelp.html).

Project Runeberg
http://runeberg.org

Project Runeberg was created and is maintained by Lysator, an academic computer society located at Linköping University in Sweden, for the purpose of collecting Nordic literature on the Web. If you long to read Strindberg in his original Swedish, or peruse any of those old Icelandic sagas, this is the place for you.

Electronic Text Collections in Western European Literature
www.lib.virginia.edu/wess/etexts.html

The Western European Studies Section of the Association of College and Research Libraries has gathered this collection of links to literary texts in western European languages other than English. Readers of Catalan, rejoice!

Le Châteux: Le Salon de la Littérature Française
www.le-chateau.ilias.com

Download the classics of French literature in their original language. These zipped files require a decompression program in order to read them. PC-users might use the free "Zip Reader" program from PKWARE (www.pkware.com/satellite-o/free_ zip_program. php). Mac-users can use the free "Stuffit Expander" (www.stuffit. com/mac/expander/index.html) to open up a new font file.

Contemporary Nonfiction

Have you heard that the U.S. government invented the Internet and then devoted all kinds of resources to feeding its quality data to it? Yep. The Feds offer over 30 million pages of government information, reports, services, and online transactions. Not only that, but they intend to make it available for time immemorial. No ephemeral Web sites here. All of this valuable free information can be searched via the portal FirstGov.gov (www.firstgov.gov).

Our taxpayer dollars are at work through the universities, too. They generously collect and lovingly disseminate archives and modern works of scholarship for all our erudition.

National Academies Press
www.nap.edu

The National Academies (of Sciences, of Engineering, the Institute of Medicine, and the National Research Council) have come together to offer the full text of over 2,000 modern scientific books online in "Open Book" format. The Open Book page image is a free, browseable, nonproprietary, fully searchable version of publications. National Academy Press subject areas include urban transportation, medicine, public health, and chemistry. Read these publications on your computer or pay to have print copies sent to you.

GrayLIT Network: A Science Portal of Technical Reports
www.osti.gov/graylit

"Gray literature" is defined as "foreign or domestic open source material that usually is available through specialized channels and may not enter normal channels or systems of publication." These are things like NASA Jet Propulsion Lab Reports and documents from the EPA.

Country Studies: Area Handbook Series
http://lcweb2.loc.gov/frd/cs/

Need to find a bit of the history of the lesser-known countries of the world? You won't find a more complete source than the Country Studies from the Federal Research Division of the Library of Congress. This database is the electronic version of hardcopy studies published between 1986 and 1998. Funding for this series was discontinued in the late 1990s, so the studies are now a bit dated. They are still valuable for student reports and such. From Azerbaijan to the United Arab Emirates, visit these studies to learn the history, geography, and recent government status of 101 countries.

University of California Press E-Editions
www.ucpress.edu/scan

The UC Press and the UC Berkeley Library have joined forces to publish the full text of nearly 1,400 online editions of modern works of scholarship, about 400 of which are available to the general public. The works fall under the following subjects: International Studies, Classics, Literature, History, Anthropology, Politics, and Religious Studies.

History and Law

The Internet is an ideal medium for distributing old or obscure material that would be hard to get otherwise. Here are some great resources in the history of law and the humanities.

Making of America: MOA
www.hti.umich.edu/m/moagrp

Here you will find a digital library of primary sources in American social history from before the Civil War through reconstruction. The collection is particularly strong in the subject areas of education, psychology, American history, sociology, religion, and science and technology. My personal favorite? *Leaves from an Actor's Note-Book, Reminiscences and Chit-Chat of the Green Room and the Stage* by actor George Vandenhoff, published in 1860. Reading it is like listening to 150-year-old gossip.

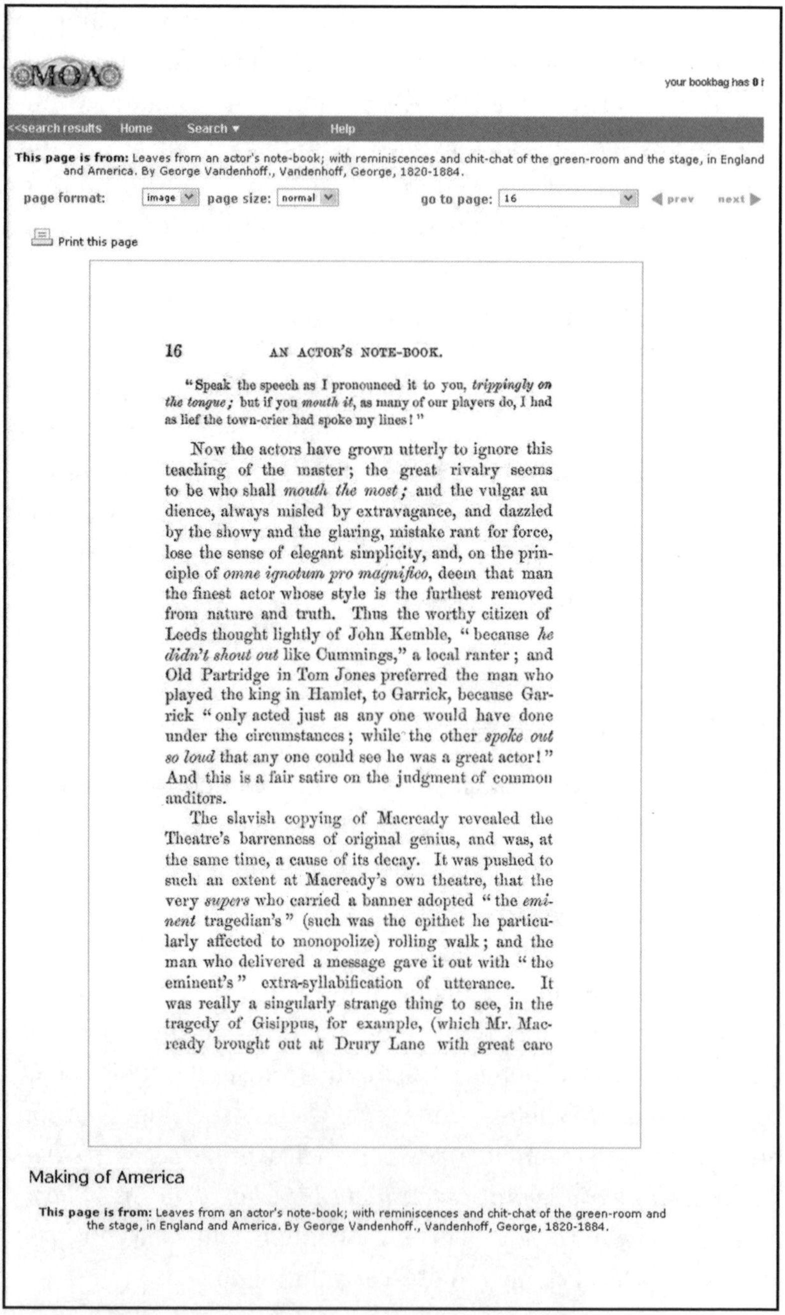

MOA

your bookbag has 0 i

<<search results   Home   Search ▼   Help

This page is from: Leaves from an actor's note-book; with reminiscences and chit-chat of the green-room and the stage, in England and America. By George Vandenhoff., Vandenhoff, George, 1820-1884.

page format: [image ▼] page size: [normal ▼]   go to page: [16   ▼] ◀ prev   next ▶

🖶 Print this page

---

16   AN ACTOR'S NOTE-BOOK.

"Speak the speech as I pronounced it to you, *trippingly on the tongue;* but if you *mouth it,* as many of our players do, I had as lief the town-crier had spoke my lines!"

Now the actors have grown utterly to ignore this teaching of the master; the great rivalry seems to be who shall *mouth the most;* and the vulgar au dience, always misled by extravagance, and dazzled by the showy and the glaring, mistake rant for force, lose the sense of elegant simplicity, and, on the prin- ciple of *omne ignotum pro magnifico,* deem that man the finest actor whose style is the furthest removed from nature and truth. Thus the worthy citizen of Leeds thought lightly of John Kemble, "because *he didn't shout out* like Cummings," a local ranter ; and Old Partridge in Tom Jones preferred the man who played the king in Hamlet, to Garrick, because Gar- rick "only acted just as any one would have done under the circumstances; while the other *spoke out so loud* that any one could see he was a great actor!" And this is a fair satire on the judgment of common auditors.

The slavish copying of Macready revealed the Theatre's barrenness of original genius, and was, at the same time, a cause of its decay. It was pushed to such an extent at Macready's own theatre, that the very *supers* who carried a banner adopted "the *emi- nent* tragedian's" (such was the epithet he particu- larly affected to monopolize) rolling walk; and the man who delivered a message gave it out with "the eminent's" extra-syllabification of utterance. It was really a singularly strange thing to see, in the tragedy of Gisippus, for example, (which Mr. Mac- ready brought out at Drury Lane with great care

---

Making of America

This page is from: Leaves from an actor's note-book; with reminiscences and chit-chat of the green-room and the stage, in England and America. By George Vandenhoff., Vandenhoff, George, 1820-1884.

Figure 6.3   Visit MOA to get the green room gossip of 1860.

Human Rights Library: University of Minnesota
www1.umn.edu/humanrts

Even if the guys who originally signed these things don't remember what's in them, *we* can find out by searching this collection of the most important international human rights treaties ever agreed to. Get them in French, Spanish, Russian, and Arabic, too.

Avalon Project at the Yale Law School
www.yale.edu/lawweb/avalon/avalon.htm

Go straight to the source with this collection of international documents "relevant to the fields of Law, History, Economics, Politics, Diplomacy, and Government." The documents are grouped by century. See also Project DIANA: An Online Human Rights Archive at this same location for the text of treaties old and new concerning the preservation of human rights.

EuroDocs
http://library.byu.edu/~rdh/eurodocs

The premier directory of links to Western European historical documents comes straight out of Brigham Young University in Provo, Utah. That's where the Harold B. Lee Library European studies bibliographer Richard Hacken created and maintains this world-class resource. Get your links to the history of Monaco and even Vatican City here—but don't expect to find all the results in English.

Internet History Sourcebooks Project (IHSP)
www.fordham.edu/halsall

Paul Halsall, now assistant professor of history at the University of North Florida, developed and edits this collection of public domain historical texts at Fordham University in New York, where he earned his PhD. The IHSP is divided into three main categories: ancient, medieval, and modern history. Additional theme areas include African, East Asian, Indian, Islamic, Jewish, women's, gay/lesbian, and global history, as well as the history of science.

U.S. Historical Documents
www.law.ou.edu/hist

The University of Oklahoma College of Law houses this site, created by Eric A. Cooper and maintained by James P. Callison. Come here for quick copies of the Monroe Doctrine, the Iroquois Constitution, and the Japanese surrender documents of World War II.

World War II Primary Source Document Collection
www.ibiblio.org/pha

Larry W. Jewell and his Pearl Harbor Working Group want to "keep the record straight" about World War II by offering the full text of documents leading up to and produced during the conflicts. Jewell especially emphasizes the attack on Pearl Harbor. He offers a special archive containing more than 5,000 items about that event.

Liberty Library of Constitutional Classics
www.constitution.org/liberlib.htm

Jon Roland sees violations of the U.S. Constitution everywhere. Because of this belief, he has mounted this full-text collection of classic books and other works on constitutional government for all to read. Take advantage of Roland's paranoia and peruse the *Code of Hammurabi*, the works of ancient Greek authors, and the *Magna Carta* in several formats. Access also the seminal works of the U.S. government, in HTML, plain text, or image files.

Religion-Online
www.religion-online.org

Religious scholar William F. Fore established this site to make major works of religions available to his divinity students at the United Theological College in Bangalore, India. Browse this extensive collection through a subject directory that covers the major issues faced by religion today. Explore writings about the Bible, of course, but also modern ethics, social issues, and practical theology (read: mental health counseling). Fore presents the full texts of writings "presenting many different points of view, but all written from the perspective of sound scholarship."

Christian Classics Ethereal Library
www.ccel.org

Harry Plantinga, professor of computer science at Calvin College, provides full-text access to the "most important public domain Christian books for theological study and ministry." Some of the works are available in other languages, especially Russian. Search the database by author, title, or type of work. And don't miss Jonathan Edwards' *Sinners in the Hands of an Angry God* (1741) in Traditional Chinese font.

Classics in the History of Psychology
http://psychclassics.yorku.ca

Christopher D. Green, a professor in the Department of Psychology at York University in Toronto, Canada, developed this full-text collection of "historically significant public domain documents from the scholarly literature of psychology and allied disciplines." It currently contains over 25 books and more than 150 articles and chapters online. The site also links to nearly 200 relevant works posted at other sites. Browse the collection by author or topic, or perform a Boolean search.

Full-Text Articles on the Open Web

Until recently, journals and magazines have been able to fetch a good price for digital copies of their current content. That is why so little of it has been available on the open Web.

Still, that situation is changing. There is a new movement afoot called "Open Access." It attempts to put "peer-reviewed scientific and scholarly literature on the Internet … free of charge and free of most copyright and licensing restrictions," thus "removing the barriers to serious research," according to Peter Suber, research professor at Earlham College in Richmond, Indiana (www.earlham. edu/~peters/fos/2004_03_07_fosblogarchive.html#a10791180794 1732035).

OAIster

http://oaister.umdl.umich.edu/o/oaister

The University of Michigan's Digital Library Production Service has assembled this outstanding collection of "freely available, previously difficult-to-access, academically-oriented digital resources that are easily searchable by anyone," according to the site. They have developed a proprietary "middleware" application that performs real-time searches of academic databases invisible to regular search engines. In effect, that makes OAIster a virtual unified search interface of open access, high-quality articles and Web sites from almost 400 academic institutions from around the world. Browse institutional databases by title or search the whole danged thing by keyword or in a delineated field search. This site is a treasure for all libraries.

Google Scholar

http://scholar.google.com

"Stand on the shoulders of giants," reads the tag line for this beta Google search service. Google Scholar combs peer-reviewed journals, books, abstracts, preprints, theses, and technical reports—in other words, scholarly information available across the Web from all areas of research. Relevance ranking on Google Scholar takes into account not only the full text of each piece but also how often it has been cited in academic literature. No doubt the usefulness of this database will increase as scholarly publication moves toward open access. Google Scholar also incorporates Google's access to scholarly books through OCLC's Open WorldCat, letting users click on "Library Search" to locate the nearest library holding the book.

FindArticles.com

www.findarticles.com

Search articles from thousands of magazines, journals, news sources, and other publications, featuring current issues and archives dating back to 1984. Some are offered full text for free. Others show abstracts with links for purchase of the full text.

MagPortal.com
www.magportal.com

Hot Neuron LLC (http://hotneuron.com) brings us this free full-text magazine site. MagPortal.com scans publishers' Web sites for free content and then adds this to its collection. The search engine allows users to sort results by date, subject, and journal name. It also allows a fuzzy kind of search for "similar" articles. Because all the content was freely available in the first place, the information on MagPortal.com tends to be of the PR release type.

E-Resources Search: Penn Library
www.library.upenn.edu/cgi-bin/res/sr.cgi

Browse the subject categories of the University of Pennsylvania Library electronic journals directory to find the serials available to users outside the Penn community. Look for the "Unrestricted Access" note below the electronic journal citation.

HighWire Press
http://highwire.stanford.edu

The Stanford University Libraries are trying to wrest some control over academic publishing away from outrageously expensive commercial publishers by linking to all the online sites that provide access to full-text articles in science for free. HighWire Press, the Internet imprint of the Stanford University Libraries, develops and maintains the Web versions of important journals in biomedicine and other disciplines. Check out their list of journals with free full-text articles online.

Medscape
www.medscape.com/px/urlinfo

In return for a free registration, gain access to full-text articles with the latest medical news in 25 specialty areas.

Full Up to Here with Full-Text Online?

Where is this free full text on the Web movement heading? Pioneers like Michael S. Hart at Project Gutenberg keep generating those out-of-copyright e-texts. At last count, he figures he has distributed digitized books worth one trillion dollars, had they been printed on paper. Project Gutenberg welcomes the keyboarding and editing efforts of volunteers. To learn more, visit Project Gutenberg: How to Volunteer (www.promo.net/pg/volunteer.hml.).

Project Gutenberg digitizes books the old fashioned way: by keying them into a computer. New technologies have made it cost-effective to scan entire books and to use optical character recognition to index them. This technology supports the Amazon.com feature "Search Inside the Book." In the program, participating publishers agree to have their books scanned and indexed by Amazon. After that, any general book query will not only retrieve bibliographic information but also phrases and words from within the text of a book. These are displayed in context on an image of the book page, along with access to the page before and after it. Because the snippet is small and is offered with permission, Amazon.com has been able to remain on the right side of the United States copyright provision for "fair use."

Google plans to push these boundaries to the limit with its "Google Book Search" (http://books.google.com) program. Google books will scan and make freely available on the Web two categories of books: in-print books with purchase links, and books from five of the world's great libraries—Oxford, Harvard, Stanford, University of Michigan, and the New York Public Library.

Google's intention is positive: to increase sales of new books and to offer access to older material that is hard to get in its printed form. For information that is no longer copyrighted, Google will even display the full text online. Unfortunately, many, if not most, of the books Google is planning to digitize may still be under copyright. In the United States, the copyright on a book published after 1923 persists, even if it goes out of print. Then the rights usually revert from the publisher to the author. That being the case, Google should negotiate with the copyright holder for permission to digitize and display any work not in the public domain.

At this writing, the legal status of the material in the Google Book Search database has not been settled. This conflict is just another example of competition between commercial forces (in this case, the publishing industry) and the World Wide Web, where information wants to be free.

The links in this chapter aren't a comprehensive list of all free full-text resources available online. Still, it should get you started. If that classic text that your patron needs is checked out, or the library is closed and a student has a paper due the next morning, these Web-based books and articles can be a great help.

Chapter 7

Health and Medical Information Online

The resident was nervous. "Umm. I think the surgeon had better discuss the pathology report with you," he said to my friend. Then he scuttled out of the room like a cockroach caught in the glare of a midnight kitchen light.

A minute later, the surgeon burst in, far too boisterous and avuncular for the occasion. It was obvious that he was uncomfortable with the outcome of his "curative" surgery. "The cancer invaded multiple nodes—we'd prefer it were fewer nodes. In fact, we'd prefer that there were no nodal involvement at all. We will have to watch you like a hawk, my friend …"

My dear companion. I had come to rely on him as a rock of strength. Yet, here he was, a fit, youthful 43 years old—with a metastatic colon cancer slipping through his lymph nodes.

What could I do? I flew to the Web, where I knew the latest research results awaited me. First, I crashed into the National Cancer Institute (www.cancer.gov) from the National Institutes of Health. There, I learned that my buddy's cancer, stage three with N2 nodal involvement, had about a 20 to 30 percent five-year survival rate. Later, doctors found that his cancer had spread to his liver. In that case, his chances of five-year survival dropped to less than 5 percent.

A little learning can be a dangerous thing. I clicked around a little bit more and came across a wonderful essay by Stephen Jay Gould, the late Harvard evolutionary biologist who, in 1982, survived abdominal mesothelioma, a rare and serious cancer.

(Twenty years later, he died of a completely different cancer, metastatic adenocarcinoma of the lung.) His words pulled me back from despair and encouraged me to find *more* information on the Web that could alter my companion's dire prognosis.

In his essay, "The Median Isn't the Message," (www.cancer guide.org/median_not_msg.html), Gould emphasized the fallacy of prognosis statistics. "Means and medians are the abstractions. ... Variation is the hard reality. None of us are average—we all vary from the mean. Also, disease prognosis statistical distributions tend to be 'right skewed,' that is, with a lower boundary of zero, i.e., discovery of the disease at death, one half of the deaths are scrunched up between a prognosis of zero years to five and the median. On the other side of the graph, a long tail stretches out, indicating the long lives of the folks who survived their disease."

My friend is young. Most people who get this cancer are above retirement age. Their life spans are limited regardless of their disease. They skew the statistical distribution down toward zero. Also, clinical trials with experimental protocols can take one out of the statistical distribution completely. Further Web research indicated that the standard chemotherapy for colon cancer increases the five-year survival rate about 30 percent. New adjuvant treatments in clinical trials increase survival chances even more.

Gould noted that a positive attitude aids in fighting cancer and other diseases. When he got sick, he did the research, made certain he got the best treatment, and interpreted the statistics correctly. "I knew how to read the data properly and not despair," he writes. "I am convinced that it played a major role in saving my life. Knowledge is power, in Bacon's proverb."

Judy Consales, Director of the Biomedical Library at the University of California at Los Angeles, concurs. "When patients are informed about their diseases and treatments, their healthcare progresses better."

She has seen a tremendous increase in patient knowledge since the dawn of the World Wide Web. "The Web has made medical information so much more accessible," she points out. She noted that the Biomedical Library, built to supply physicians with the latest medical findings, is considering altering its charter. With so much medical information available on the Web, the library feels it might need to expand its emphasis from professional information to consumer education.

General Medical Information

Craig Haynes, head of the Medical Center Library at the University of California, San Diego, states, "Presently, there are scores of nationally recognized, peer-reviewed, professional healthcare associations and government agencies with a clear and defining presence on the Web. Many of these sites are specifically targeted to the consumer health client. These professionally maintained and reviewed healthcare sites offer consumers the best when it comes to basic health information.

"Health information acquired from these reputable sites do at least two important things. First of all, they equip the consumer with basic knowledge regarding a desired health behavior or an existing health condition. Secondly, when used in consultation with a qualified health professional, the information the consumer gleans from a reputable Web site can open a dialogue between patient and caregiver; and that is a very important element in both diagnosis and treatment."

A word of caution, though. In June 2001, a healthy 24-year-old woman volunteer in an asthma study at Johns Hopkins University died because a chemical given her to inhale caused the progressive failure of her lungs and kidneys. It seems that the doctor conducting his own online searches overlooked numerous citations in medical literature about the dangers of inhaling the chemical hexamethonium.

In this case, it appears that a medical librarian, trained in the intricacies of MEDLINE, could have alerted the doctors to the danger and helped to prevent the woman's death. The moral of the story? If you need a complete literature search on a dangerous or rare health question, consult a skilled medical librarian.

On the other hand, when a patron comes in and wants more information on her niece's recently diagnosed Ehlers Danlos syndrome, say, you can easily get the general outlines of the current information on the disease or condition from the Web. Here are some resources.

The Merck Manual of Diagnosis and Therapy
www.merck.com/mrkshared/mmanual/home.jsp

When doctors and nurses get sick, they turn to this standard of diagnosis. Merck offers its 17th edition, completely revised in 1999 but constantly updated, online for free. Completely searchable, this online publication lists the causes, symptoms, and prognosis of just about everything that can go wrong with you. It also covers mental conditions, pediatrics, and infectious disease. Reading disease descriptions in the Merck, I always start to feel a little funny, as if I were developing the symptoms of all the ailments in the book.

Figure 7.1   Look to the Merck Manual to find out what ails you.

The Merck Manual Second Home Edition
www.merck.com/mmhe/index.html

Do users find medical terms in the regular Merck Manual too incomprehensible? Search the Second Home Edition for the same great information translated into terms that all of us can understand. This site is a terrific tool for students writing reports on diseases.

MayoClinic.com
www.mayoclinic.com

The famous Mayo Clinic in Minnesota offers reliable, general information about a variety of ailments and conditions. In addition to clear information about disease, MayoClinic.com offers healthy lifestyle planners. Get started today reducing stress, stopping smoking, and getting your weight under control. This is a great place to start.

Aetna InteliHealth
www.intelihealth.com/IH/ihtIH

Experts at Harvard Medical School provide most of the searchable content for Aetna InteliHealth. This site aims to offer a collection of consumer health information from the best possible sources. Value-added features include patient drug information, interactive health tools, and risk assessments. Funding comes from Aetna, a health insurance company.

MEDLINEplus Health Information
http://medlineplus.gov

The National Library of Medicine has assembled its resources onto one attractive portal designed for general health consumers. Search for information on conditions, diseases, drugs, and wellness. Use the medical dictionary to translate incomprehensible medical terms. You may also jump directly from this site to ClinicalTrials.gov, the medical research program from the National Institutes of Health.

Centers for Disease Control and Prevention (CDC)
www.cdc.gov

This is the leading U.S. federal agency for protecting health and safety. Visit the CDC to learn about emerging infectious diseases, various diseases and conditions, and other health and safety topics.

Internet Mental Health
www.mentalhealth.com

While treating the body, don't forget the mind. Canadian psychiatrist Phillip W. Long, MD runs this resource that offers very complete mental health information. Get the scoop on common mental disorders and psychotropic medication here. Long offers self-diagnostic psychology tests on his companion site, MyTherapy.com (www.mytherapy.com/features) for a modest fee. This is a great place to start for handling all kinds of mental unhappiness.

Familydoctor.org
http://familydoctor.org

The American Academy of Family Physicians (www.aafp.org) offers this searchable directory of consumer health information on the wide variety of conditions and ailments that a family doctor might encounter. Some of the information is also available in Spanish. Users can search by symptom to get a head start on diagnosing themselves.

Disease Directories

Now that you have the basics on what ails you, you might want to explore the breadth of information on what to do next. You can get an idea of the number and quality of sites dedicated to your condition by checking these directories.

Emory MedWeb
www.medweb.emory.edu/MedWeb/default.htm

The staff of the Robert W. Woodruff Health Sciences Center Library of Emory University created this directory designed to support the work of their medical students and researchers as well as the general public. Use their directory to browse such subjects as "Consumer Health" or "Drug Interactions," or search the database by keyword.

HealthWeb
http://healthweb.org/index.cfm

This directory of quality health resources stems from a collaborative effort between the Library of the Health Sciences at the University of Illinois at Chicago and the Committee on Institutional Cooperation's "HealthWeb" project. Click on a general ailment category to find links to all the major Web portals sites that address an issue.

Hardin MD: Medical Information + Pictures
www.lib.uiowa.edu/hardin/md

Eric Rumsey compiled this site for the Hardin Library for the Health Sciences at the University of Iowa. He writes, "As the name 'meta directory' implies, Hardin MD is a 'list of lists.'" Its purpose is to provide easy access to comprehensive resource lists in health-related subjects. Hardin MD also has links to medical pictures, so users can see what a brown recluse spider's bite looks like, for instance.

Librarians' Index to the Internet Health & Medicine:
Diseases & Conditions
http://lii.org/search/file/diseases_and_conditions

The incomparable LII brings you this extensive list of links to annotated site selections, chosen by librarians. If LII lists it, you know it is an interesting and reliable resource.

Yahoo! Directory Health: Diseases and Conditions
http://dir.yahoo.com/health/diseases_and_conditions

No matter what your complaint (including shyness), find Web resources about it here in Yahoo!'s comprehensive list.

In-Depth Resources and Literature

When dealing with a cost-conscious HMO, you've got to know what is wrong with you, you've got to know the latest treatment for it, and then you've got to demand it from your provider. Use these resources to find the latest research developments for your symptoms.

Medscape.com
www.medscape.com/px/urlinfo

Designed for clinicians as well as consumers, Medscape.com offers the Web's largest collection of free, full-text clinical medicine articles enhanced with keyword searches, graphics, annotated links to Internet resources, and more. Browse 29 specialty areas and sign up for free e-mail newsletters. This site is free, but requires registration.

PubMed Central
www.pubmedcentral.gov

Need a full-text biomedical journal article? Search PubMed Central, the U.S. National Library of Medicine's free digital archive of biomedical and life sciences journal literature. "PubMed Central aims to fill the role of a world class library in the digital age," according to the site. It will become the repository of choice for the freely available fruits of biomedical research funded by the National Institutes of Health, reputed to fund as much as a quarter of the world's best medical research. And that is only the beginning. It even contains all the material in the peer-reviewed BioMed Central database (www.biomedcentral.com).

PubMed
www.ncbi.nlm.nih.gov/entrez/query.fcgi/

The National Library of Medicine maintains the premier bibliographic database covering the fields of medicine, nursing, dentistry, and veterinary medicine. Called MEDLINE, this resource contains bibliographic citations and author abstracts for more than 15 million biomedical articles dating back to the 1950s. Use the PubMed interface to search for abstracts of the latest research on what ails you. When you find a promising citation, click on the "Related Articles" link. PubMed will automatically search to find more listings relevant to your search. Warning: These articles are written in "research-ese" and so can be difficult to understand. Keep a medical dictionary on hand at all times for the translation.

NLM Gateway

http://gateway.nlm.nih.gov/gw/Cmd

The NLM Gateway lets users search simultaneously in multiple retrieval systems at the U.S. National Library of Medicine (NLM). It provides "one-stop searching" for many of NLM's information resources or databases. Use this site to search not only MEDLINE, but also AIDS Meetings, DIRLINE, OLDMEDLINE, and others.

Other Medical Resources

These medical dictionaries can help translate medical terms into English. Also, some of these sites can provide details about the medicine the doctor prescribed for you.

American Medical Association

www.ama-assn.org

This site features some full-text articles from the *Journal of the American Medical Association* (*JAMA*) and a Doctor Finder (http://dbapps.ama-assn.org/aps/amahg.htm) with basic professional information on virtually every licensed physician in the United States. Search for a doctor by name or specialty. See where the doctor went to school and how long he or she has been in the profession.

AIM DocFinder

www.docboard.org/docfinder.html

The Association of State Medical Board Executive Directors offers this list of state medical licensing authorities. Choose your state then look up your doctor to see if he or she has come under censure.

InteliHealth: Merriam-Webster Medical Dictionary

www.intelihealth.com/IH/ihtIH/WSIPN000/9276/
9276.html?

Just what is "adipose tissue," anyway? Find out using the online version of the Merriam-Webster Medical Dictionary, brought to you by Aetna InteliHealth.

PDR Health

www.pdrhealth.com/drug_info/index.html

The Physician's Desk Reference (PDR) is where doctors turn to decide what medicine to give you. Access to the professional version of this resource requires a fee. Still, the consumer portal for this information is searchable for free. Use this database to learn what medical professionals know about the drugs that you are taking.

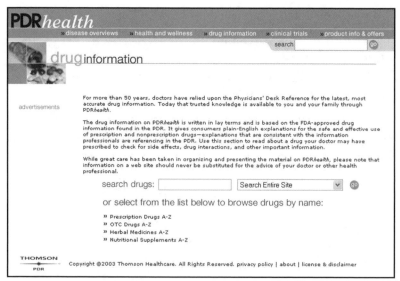

**Figure 7.2   What's that medicine? Search the consumer portal from the
Physician's Desk Reference to find out.**

RxList.com

www.rxlist.com

This Internet drug index was founded and is maintained by Neil Sandow, PharmD, director of pharmacy for several San Francisco area hospitals. RxList lets you search by drug name, imprint code, or keyword, then offers hyperlink access to Taber's Medical Encyclopedia from the results page.

HerbMed

www.herbmed.org

Do clinical trials demonstrate that echinacea, St. John's wort, or saw palmetto actually work? Here's a site that separates fact from folklore. Browse the Alternative Medicine Foundation's alphabetical catalog of medicinal herbs to see what science has to say about these unregulated biochemical substances.

Lab Tests Online

www.labtestsonline.org

Your mom just got her CBC test results back. What is that? And what do the results mean? Visit this site for lab test information by disease, test name, or screening population group. Find out which routine tests you should undergo and how often. Check out the category on this site called "In the News" that gives the latest medical test research results.

Health Insurance Consumer Guides

www.healthinsuranceinfo.net

As health care costs soar, fewer people can afford health insurance. The Georgetown University Health Policy Institute has written a set of 51 consumer guides for getting and keeping health insurance, one for each state and the District of Columbia. They are available, updated, and free at this Web site. The guides provide overviews of state aids in obtaining health insurance.

Cancer: What Is It Good For?

What's cancer good for? Absolutely nothing! All right, I admit that I am a bit fixated on the topic. Still, so many of us have cancer or love people who have been made sick or died from it. Cancer *stinks* (to use the polite term), whether or not it eventually kills you. Use these links to find support and, perhaps, a cure. Many of these same kinds of online resources are available for many calamitous diseases, especially AIDS, heart disease, and multiple sclerosis. Search MedlinePlus (http://medlineplus.gov) for listings of major support groups for particular diseases or conditions.

National Cancer Institute
www.cancer.gov

This site from the National Institutes of Health is the most current, credible, and comprehensive information center about cancer available on the Web. Most of the information on the National Cancer Institute (NCI) site comes from PDQ, NCI's comprehensive cancer database. NCI offers information about all the different types of treatment for cancer, clinical trials, genetics, causes, risk factors, prevention, testing, coping, and more.

American Society for Clinical Oncology (ASCO)
www.asco.org

Here, oncologists worldwide share their latest findings. Look here to find a specialist in your particular cancer. Also, search the article database for abstracts about the results of the latest experimental treatments.

OncoLink
http://oncolink.upenn.edu

Located at the University of Pennsylvania, OncoLink is often cited as one of the best resources anywhere on the Web. Although much of the physician-specific information is copied directly from the NCI site, it is presented in a way that makes it sometimes faster and easier to navigate. The patient-specific information on the financial aspects of cancer treatment and the frequently asked questions section is exceptional. It provides a large collection of links to support groups, peer-reviewed journals, hospitals, and other online references.

American Cancer Society
www.cancer.org

The American Cancer Society (ACS) site targets the most common cancer types, such as lung, breast, and colon. It features modules on prostate and breast cancer.

National Coalition for Cancer Survivorship (NCCS)
www.canceradvocacy.org

The National Coalition for Cancer Survivorship, a nonprofit support organization, sponsors this portal that brings together psychosocial resources for cancer patients and their families by providing links to Web sites around the world. The section describing clinical trials is very well done and would help any patient with newly diagnosed cancer.

Clinical Trials

Sometimes the regular treatment for cancer or other diseases just won't work. This was the case with my friend, whose metastatic cancer, treated traditionally, would surely kill him. In that situation, it pays to volunteer for a research protocol, that is, a clinical trial that admits you into the newest experimental treatments. Not only does this path represent your best chance for a cure, but you help others, too, by advancing the research process.

ClinicalTrials.gov
www.clinicaltrials.gov

The National Institutes of Health, through its National Library of Medicine, has developed ClinicalTrials.gov to provide patients, family members, and members of the public current information about clinical research studies. Browse trials by broad disease

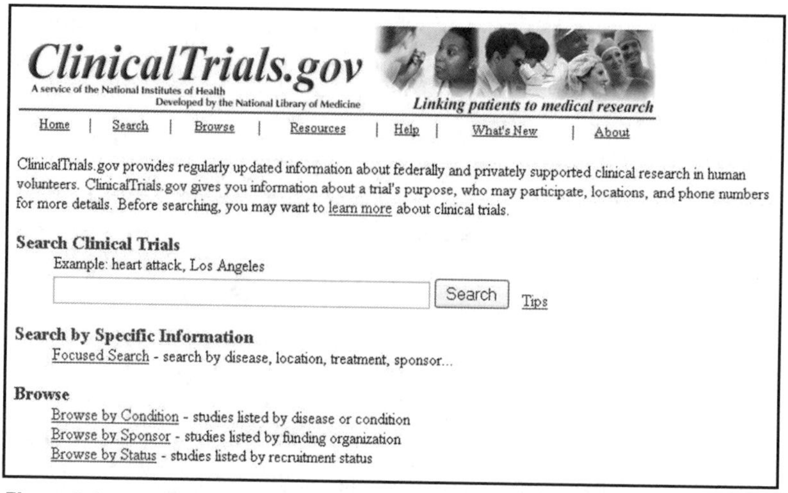

Figure 7.3   Find a cutting-edge clinical trial through the National Institutes of Health.

heading or alphabetically by precise condition. Or do a focused search that allows you to limit by geographical location.

CenterWatch Clinical Trials Listing Service
http://centerwatch.com

Use this site to find information related to a variety of clinical trials, as well as new drug therapies recently approved by the FDA. CenterWatch also offers a patient notification service in which you will receive an e-mail when a new clinical trial in your area of interest is submitted, or when the FDA approves new drugs that might fit your profile. Use this site as an adjunct to ClinicalTrials.gov.

National Cancer Institute: Clinical Trials
http://cancer.gov/clinical_trials

Search for a cancer clinical trial on this National Cancer Institute database. Query by cancer type, treatment type, clinical trial phase, and, most important, by geographic location. Get contact information for the nation's experts in your type of cancer. Call these experts and ask them what to do.

Quack Attack

As Director at the Biomedical Library at the University of California at Los Angeles, Judy Consales is concerned about unscrupulous medical Web sites. Some sites offer false or unproven information. Others, such as "find the best doctor" sites, often charge for their services. "People in their zeal spend money unnecessarily." These two sites keep an eye on healthcare fraud:

National Council against Health Fraud (NCAHF)
www.ncahf.org

The NCAHF is a nonprofit, tax-exempt voluntary health agency comprised of health professionals, educators, researchers, attorneys, and concerned citizens. This private, nonpolitical, and non-sectarian organization works against health fraud, misinformation, and quackery as public health problems. The NCAHF site features newsletters and position papers. It is searchable.

Quackwatch: Your Guide to Health Fraud Quackery
www.quackwatch.org

Dr. Stephen Barrett maintains this extensive site, which includes articles, consumer protection alerts, and links to other anti-quackery sites. Barrett is the dean of today's anti-quackery movement in the U.S.

Craig Haynes, head of the Medical Center Library at the University of California at San Diego, is hopeful about the medical information available on the Web. "Over the last two years or so, the quality of health information available to consumers via the World Wide Web has greatly improved. While there is still a lot of inaccurate and patently unscientific medical information out there, that situation has been countered with the availability of more reputable information."

How can you judge the quality of Web health sites? Basically, the same way librarians judge the quality of any resource. Who wrote the page and what are his or her credentials? Is the information on the page current and complete enough for your needs? Is the purpose of the site educational or commercial?

There is an organization that puts its imprimatur on Web pages that supply health and medical information. The Health On the Net Foundation (www.hon.ch), a nonprofit organization headquartered in Geneva, Switzerland, was created with the support of tele-medicine experts and major medical institutions in Europe, Asia, and the Americas to build and support the international health and medical community on the Internet and World Wide Web. The Foundation has developed eight ethical management principles for healthcare Web site developers, including the criteria that healthcare professionals supply the site's information and that the site clearly acknowledge the source of funding. Look for the "HONcode" seal of approval on medical Web pages as an assurance of quality.

The Health On the Net Foundation makes its Code of Conduct available on the Web in 17 languages (www.hon.ch/HONcode/Conduct.html). Learn and teach these critical standards for judging medical information on the Web. These standards can mean the difference between finding lifesaving information and bogus nonsense that can cause harm, or even death.

A Long Struggle

After that visit to the surgeon, my friend's troubles really began.

Using the databases listed in this chapter, I found a clinical trial for him that gave him a 50 percent chance of surviving his otherwise fatal disease. Problem? His HMO wouldn't pay for the treatment outside their facilities. Although the HMO's decision spelled certain death for him, they were legally correct in denying him treatment. After all, your insurance company only promises to make you well if it determines statistically that you can get well.

Under our current healthcare system, the desperately ill often must choose between losing their life or their life savings.

Still, even a giant HMO is no match for a determined librarian.

I got a hold of my state senator. He just happened to be working on HMO reform legislation at that very moment. He called the HMO and informed them of his concern over my cohort's plight. Within three weeks, the HMO agreed to pay for my friend's chemotherapy, a cost that would otherwise have left him bankrupt.

The good news: The chemotherapy worked, dissolving every trace of the evil intruder. Thanks to research, persistence, and luck, my chum is alive and well today. What a relief.

Remember, no Web site can replace the relationship between a patient and a doctor. Still, good quality, current medical information gleaned from the Web can improve the doctor/patient relationship and make both aware of new lifesaving treatments becoming available every day. I hope they serve you and your patrons as well as they did my friend!

Chapter 8

Minding Your Money on the Web

For a few years in the late 1990s, the stock market went nowhere but up. "Irrational exuberance," Alan Greenspan called it. Then came the "correction," the jarring plummet of stock prices that wiped out so many dot-coms. Major corporate fraud such as that committed by Enron, accompanied by corrupt practices from its accounting firm, Arthur Andersen, left investors wondering whom they could trust. Now, in the middle of the first decade of the 21st century, the market is slowly recovering, although many American workers are losing their jobs to "off-shoring." How is the average investor to prosper in these tricky times?

Financial resources and advice pervade the Web, even during financial down times. The biggest difficulty for the lay-investor is finding a good jumping off point, a site that offers solid information in a comfortable and easy-to-use format.

Only two types of Web pages have been able to get away with charging for access—pornography and financial information sites. Don't ask me about the relationship between the two. I think it has something to do with what Freud called the "Pleasure Principle."

Still, you can name your price. A few of the full-service metasites I found charge as much as $120 per year for a subscription to their services. Other sites offer nearly the same service and are utterly free. Still others, such as Value Line, offer premium information for close to $1,000 per year.

I will concentrate here on starting points useful to the "nonmillionaire" investor, although those seeking competitive intelligence may find them useful, too. This is not a complete list, merely some suggestions to get you started off right on your moneymaking day.

Financial Portals and Portfolios

Before the dot-com bust, every commercial site in America offered free e-mail accounts. If you visited the site to check your e-mail, you would also put your eyeballs on the advertising around it. When the bubble burst, ad revenue dried up, and many free e-mail accounts blew away.

Now that Internet advertising is regaining strength, a new free service is being widely offered to those who favor financial information: free Web-based portfolio trackers. When general financial and business information portals offer these trackers, users will return every day to check their stocks—and view the site.

Here are some good general investing Web sites, many of which offer a free portfolio tracking service.

Yahoo! Finance
http://finance.yahoo.com

This is a wonderful place to introduce yourself to the world of investment and personal finance. In return for free registration, get your finances in order with an amazing array of online money management tools. Users can assess their assets, pay bills, and establish portfolios. The "Mutual Fund Center" offers basic investment education as well as hot tips. The "Planning Center" helps users save and invest toward goals such as paying for college or retirement. Comparison tools for loans and insurance are here, too. On the "Investment" side, find loads of stock information and tutorials.

MSN Money
http://moneycentral.msn.com/home.asp

Microsoft and CNBC combine to offer this information-packed money management portal. Users can visit the "Investing" section

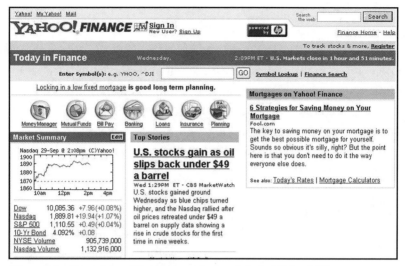

Figure 8.1 Financial neophytes can get a good start at Yahoo! Finance.

to track their investments with a personal portfolio, read stock and bond news, and read articles from CNBC. Visit the "Planning" section for articles about everything from making a budget to planning for retirement.

Reuters Business Channel
http://today.reuters.com/business/default.aspx

Serious investors can get more than 1.5 million investment Research Reports from over 700 providers, many at no cost. They can also explore Reuters' fundamental data on more than 10,000 companies. There's a lot of financial news here, along with a free portfolio tracker. All these treasures are available in return for a free registration.

SmartMoney.com
http://smartmoney.com

This is the online version of Dow Jones & Company and Hearst Communications, Inc.'s magazine of "personal business." It offers detailed coverage of financial news and markets as well as a suite of investment tools. It's also available in RSS feed. Put your portfolio here, too.

BusinessWeek Online
www.businessweek.com

This magazine is designed as a quick overview for managers on their lunch breaks. *BusinessWeek* print subscribers get access to the complete text of the magazine online. Guests get quite a bit gratis, including general financial and technology news, a global business roundup, news and tools for business school and career-building, a small business portal, and, in return for free registration, a portfolio tracker.

Value Engine
www.valuengine.com/servlet/Main

Yale finance professor Dr. Zhiwu Chen developed this mathematical computer model for analyzing stocks. Fill out a free registration for access to market overviews and news, and a valuation summary. Buy a premium pass at about $25 monthly to get detailed stock analysis and multistock comparisons.

WhisperNumber.com
www.whispernumber.com/wn_home.jsp

Forget cold analysis. Get the unofficial buzz on company earnings forecasts from WhisperNumber.com. This site compiles information from EPS, CCBN, and other financial sites. Warning—the information on this site is based on market sentiment only. Register to receive updates and news and a place to track your portfolio.

Business News and Commentary

The Wall Street Journal Online
http://online.wsj.com/public/us

Businesspeople do not consider their day to have begun properly until they have read the *Wall Street Journal* (WSJ). Stock-watching patrons at our public library whine that the library's only paper copy is always in use. Perhaps we should offer the Web version of this essential financial starting point. WSJ headlines are available to all users, but full stories are available only to subscribers of the Online Journal. For a subscription price of $79 a year, or $39 for print subscribers, the site offers up-to-date news, detailed company reports, and personalized news and quotes. WSJ Online is also available in several categorized RSS feeds.

WSJ Online offers some information gratis: career advice for professionals and college students, real estate information, tips for small business owners, columns about personal computing, and business news written in Chinese.

CBS MarketWatch
http://cbs.marketwatch.com/news

Get business news and commentary written on the page or in streaming video or audio on this handsome news portal. Have it delivered to your PDA or mobile phone. Use the tools for personal finance and investing. Register to track your portfolio. Premium commentary is available for an additional fee.

Fortune Online
www.fortune.com/fortune

CNN/Money
http://money.cnn.com

If you like to read *Fortune* and *Money*, media giant Time Warner offers versions of these magazines *in toto* for print subscribers (including annual lists such as the "100 Best Companies to Work For"), with some content free for guests.

Forbes.com: Financial News, Business News
www.forbes.com

Find Forbes financial news here then visit the blog called "Digital Tool" to read the editor's pick of the most useful article of the week.

Online Resources for Stock Trading

Uncertainties, such as oil shortages and terrorist threats, can make the stock market a lukewarm performer. Still, Peter Lynch, the former manager of the Fidelity Magellan Fund, notes that stocks are a good investment in the long term. "If you're going to get shaken out of the stock market just because of bad news, you probably don't belong in stocks in the first place," declares Lynch (Malaspina, Margaret A. "Peter Lynch: The Pitfalls of Timing the Market." *Fidelity Investor's Weekly*, July 16, 2004).

The advent of the Web and the concurrent boom in the stock market spawned the do-it-yourself investor movement. Today, although the market zigzags, online trading persists.

How can you see how your stock is doing? You must use a "ticker symbol" to get a quote for your stock. On most stock tracking sites, you can look up a ticker symbol by its company name. Then, use the ticker symbol to find the stock "quote."

The quote will reveal the time and price of the last trade made for the stock on that day, and the previous day's closing price. It will tell you the change in the stock price for the day. The stock's price-to-earnings ratio will also appear in the quote, plus a variety of other relevant information.

Major financial portals like Yahoo! Finance (http://finance.yahoo.com) offer slightly delayed stock quote information. Here are a couple of sites that specialize in quotes.

PC Quote
www.pcquote.com

Sign up for the free "My PC Quote" account for a place to put a personal portfolio and a customizable home page that can include sector trackers, watch lists, and a performance indicator based on real-time data that displays color-coded areas to show you what stocks are hot or what are not.

BigCharts
http://bigcharts.marketwatch.com

Need stock charts to track the fortunes of your investments online? Get them any way you want them at BigCharts, which also offers historical stock quotes.

ASK Research
www.askresearch.com/index.asp

Stock watchers get the numbers with a 15 to 20 minute delay for free. Sign up for premium access to get real-time information.

Mutual Funds

Value Line
www.valueline.com

Where I work, in the affluent bedroom suburb of San Marino, patrons challenge each other for the use of the venerable Value Line publication needed for monitoring mutual funds. Print subscribers can access the corresponding service online for no charge. Even so, guest users may find useful general economic commentary here for free.

Morningstar.com
www.morningstar.com

In return for a free registration, Morningstar offers a lot to the beginning investor: newsletters, an interactive site, and a portfolio monitor. "Premium Members" pay a fee for access to the complete suite of analyst research and the site's most powerful tools.

Bonds

BondsOnline: Your Source for Fixed Income Investing
www.bondsonline.com

Maybe you have grown a bit leery of the stock market. Maybe your fixed income doesn't allow you to gamble your investments away. Just click over to BondsOnline to get education and direction in making bond investment decisions. It provides articles, newsletters, and bond value calculators for the bond market investor.

BondTalk.com
www.bondtalk.com

Visit BondTalk.com to find "live talk and analysis of the bond market and the economy." This site features the research of Anthony "Tony" J. Crescenzi, a major bond market strategist.

Financial Planning

"Five years ago, self-directed financial planning advice and tools were going to make everyone the master of her own retirement, college and investment planning," writes Jeanhee Kim of Forbes.com (www.forbes.com/bow/b2c/category.jhtml?id =62). Yet, Kim notes, since the stock market drop of 2001, many more investors seek professional advice before they invest their hard-earned dough. Generally, that advice will cost you (although wisdom from a professional may well be worth it). Still, there are sites that volunteer information about how to handle your money.

Kiplinger.com: Trusted Financial Advice
www.kiplinger.com

The Kiplinger site offers business forecasts and advice on personal finances. Retirement advice, calculators, stock quotes, and more are free for use by all. Kiplinger's Tax, Agriculture, and California newsletters are considered premium content available to subscribers only.

Financial Engines
www.financialengines.com

Guests can access a wide variety of solid advice about how to build personal wealth on a modest income. Members pay $150—$300 annually for personalized advice.

About Retirement Planning
http://retireplan.about.com

Harmon W. McKinney Jr. authors this comprehensive annotated guide to online retirement planning resources. Subject areas include 401(k)s, living on a retirement income, and issues specific to women.

"How-To" Sites

I remember so well the day in the late 1990s when I urged my husband to buy a bunch of stock in the Learning Company. "They have great products," I insisted. "How can we lose?"

Two weeks later, Mattel bought the Learning Company and both of their fortunes took an instant dive. So much for my investing instincts. That's why I am a librarian, not a banker. But seriously, most of us could use some training in the complicated business of investing money. These educational resources can point us in the right direction.

Money Chimp
www.moneychimp.com

"MoneyChimp seeks to be the most coherent, logical, useful and accessible financial education resource on the face of the earth. (We're about halfway there.)" This site is simple, attractive, and easy to understand, a good place for novices to learn about investing.

Motley Fool
www.fool.com

You gotta love these guys. The Gardner brothers, Tom and David, have created a great place for investors to check in and hang out. Their venue for the wise "fools" who take financial matters into their own hands offers insightful market commentary and portfolio-enhancing stock analysis. Beginners can benefit from the "Fool's School" tutorials, and everyone can register for free to receive access to stock ideas, commentary, and a spot to hang an online portfolio. Motley Fool's message boards are very active, although visitors should beware of self-serving advice.

Value Line University
www.valueline.com/vlu/index.html

My patrons ask me, "How do I use Value Line?" If I really knew, would I be sitting behind a reference desk? No. I would be at my sea-side estate drinking margaritas. I should march these customers over to a computer and set them down in front of these free lessons from the masters of money. Students first learn investment basics. Then they learn how to establish goals and make plans to achieve them. The third lesson involves designing portfolios. Finally, students graduate after learning how to study, track, then buy and sell stocks. Sounds like it's time for me to go to online school, too!

GE Center for Financial Learning
www.financiallearning.com/ge/home.jsp

The same corporation that makes light bulbs and runs NBC also sells financial services. This site offers a free set of wonderful lessons (in return for registration) teaching how to manage and then invest our hard-earned dough. GE even gives us tips about how to deal with a sudden change in personal finances, such as the death of a wage-earning spouse.

Women's Institute for Financial Education
www.wife.org

Volunteers Candace Bahr and Ginita Wall operate this beginning-investor site designed to help women connect to resources that will help them prosper and grow financially. Their slogan? "A man is not a financial plan."

Wachowicz's Web World: Web Sites for Discerning Finance Students
http://web.utk.edu/~jwachowi/wacho_world.html

Professor John M. Wachowicz Jr. of the Department of Finance at the University of Tennessee assembled this large yet well-maintained list of annotated links of interest to finance students. The links break into eight categories: introduction to financial management, valuation, tools of financial analysis and planning, working capital management, investment in capital assets, the costs of capital, intermediate and long-term financing, and special areas of financial management. Wachowicz even provides some PowerPoint slides, so you can present what you have learned to your friends.

Company Information

When you buy stock, you are buying a company. Better check it out before you put your money down.

Hoover's Online
www.hoovers.com/free

When a patron asks for company information, I turn to Hoover's to find it. Although much of the site is gated, you can still get quite a bit of dirt on larger, public, mostly U.S.-based businesses, although some international enterprises are listed, too. Free data includes company contact information, a link to the Web site, a few original paragraphs written about the company by Hoover's editorial staff, the names of several top executives, and the names of three top competitors. Key financial numbers are here, too.

Business.com
www.business.com

Search the "Business Internet" here. Mine specific company information or drill down through their directory to information for specific industries. Browse business news or look for job openings.

Search the EDGAR Database
www.sec.gov/edgar/searchedgar/webusers.htm

"This site will allow you to retrieve publicly available filings submitted to the Securities and Exchange Commission from January

Figure 8.2 Hoover's is your first stop for company information.

1994 to the present." In other words, this site can access all the current government filings for America's public companies and mutual funds. The U.S. Securities and Exchange Commission's Electronic Data Gathering, Analysis, and Retrieval system (EDGAR) performs automated collection, indexing, and posting of the extensive reports on operations filed by all publicly held U.S.-based companies and mutual funds. SEC filings are especially useful for finding out details about a company, say, a biography of a company officer. The site offers a searching tutorial for new users. Take advantage of your tax dollars at work in cyberspace!

Advice for Investors: Canadian Company Profiles
www.fin-info.com

If you grow your money north of the border, this is the site for you. Enter a stock symbol or the name of a publicly traded Canadian company, and this site will generate a page of links to stock quotes, press releases, company Web sites, and other company information from reliable sources. The database covers companies listed on the Canadian stock exchanges, including the

Toronto Stock Exchange (TSE), the Vancouver Stock Exchange (VSE), and the Montreal Exchange (ME).

Corporate Information
www.corporateinformation.com

In return for free "trial" registration, Wright Investors Service offers access to information and ratings on world securities markets including 30,000 company profiles from 53 countries. Free access is limited to three profiles per day, although a broader subscription service is available. This is a great site for information on companies not based in the United States, although many U.S. companies have listings here, too.

Kompass.com
www1.kompass.com/kinl/index.php

Search international company information by industry, company, trade, or executive name, or mix it up in an "advanced search." Basic information is free, although more in-depth info comes at a price. Contains information about 1.8 million companies in 75 countries.

Dun & Bradstreet (D&B)
www.dnb.com/us

Access the D&B databases over the Web on a pay-per-use basis. These proprietary databases contain value-added information such as company background reports or the D&B Million Dollar Databases covering both private and public U.S. companies. Search for free to find company contact information.

Fraud Watch

Ahh, Enron. In the late 1990s, the Houston-based energy trader reigned as the seventh-biggest company (in terms of revenue) in the United States. Yet, in 2002, it was revealed that the company had overstated its profits by more than $580 million since 1997. With the complicity of its accounting firm, Arthur Andersen, it had systematically lied to everyone about how much money the company had made—and lost. Within six weeks of the fraud exposure, the once giant Enron corporation went out of business. According to CNN, "Enron's collapse left investors burned and thousands of employees out of work with lost retirement savings" ("Explaining the Enron Bankruptcy," http://archives.cnn.com/2002/US/01/12/enron.qanda.focus).

How can the average investor keep from being hornswoggled by these slick corporate varmints? Here are some sites that can help.

Bigger than Enron: Questions Investors Need to Ask
www.pbs.org/wgbh/pages/frontline/shows/regulation/etc/questions.html

A. Larry Elliott and Richard J. Schroth, management experts, note that, "Fifty percent of American households support corporations by buying stock." They say that, after Enron, individual investors "need to ask some hard, even rude, questions" about companies, their management, and their boards of directors. This site, from the television show *Frontline*, shows investors how to protect themselves.

Investor Education and Assistance
www.sec.gov/investor.shtml

The U.S. Security and Exchange Commission says, "We cannot tell you what investments to make, but we can tell you how to invest wisely and avoid fraud." Find tips and answers to common investing questions here. There is even a section to give librarians easy access to selected securities and investor information at the SEC.

The Corporate Library
www.thecorporatelibrary.com

"The Corporate Library is an independent investment research firm providing corporate governance data, analysis & risk assessment tools." Search the site for free to find quite a bit about

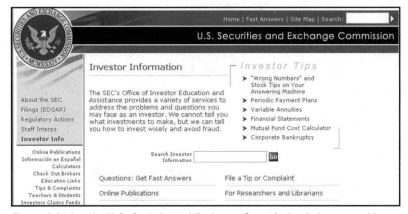

Figure 8.3   Let the U.S. Security and Exchange Commission help you avoid fraudulent investments.

selected major U.S. corporations and how they run. Subscribe to the site to learn even more.

Scandal, Inc.

http://money.cnn.com/news/specials/corruption

CNN/Money gives us this page that tracks developments related to corporate crime. Find out which corporations and accounting firms are in trouble, and why.

Free vs. Fee

As you may have noticed, many of these financial sites cost big bucks to use, while some are free. Although the old truism still holds that there is no free lunch, searchers should still "follow the money" and find out who put this information up there and why. For example, the EDGAR site, as we know, is paid for by tax dollars. Another site, EDGAR Online (www.edgar-online.com/start.asp), offers the same information for a fee, albeit with a few more searching, display, and automatic notification features added.

In another example, when companies whose business it is to sell financial services start offering free investor education, you will want to watch for possible conflicts of interest or hidden agenda. Watch out for self-aggrandizing product assessments. And make sure your clients and patrons look twice, too.

Still, the Internet offers plenty of business information that is free, accurate, and relatively unbiased. For example, if you just want to monitor the daily pulse of your stock holdings, you have your choice of sites—most of which offer direct links to commercial Web-based stock transaction sites. On the other hand, free stock quote services usually delay their reports by at least 15 minutes. So, if you are a member of that rapidly disappearing profession, the day trader, you will want to turn to paid services that serve their stock quotes in real time.

If you visit a different financial Web site every day, you could be an investing expert in a couple of months. One day, who knows? You might pass the millionaire mark. Which leaves you—and me—with only one question. If we're so smart, why ain't we rich?

Chapter 9

Let's Go Cyber-Shopping

Dot-com boom or dot-com bust, our patrons still need to buy things. And usually they want to compare the quality and prices of the goods they purchase. That is why the magazine *Consumer Reports* is so popular. In my library, this magazine has its own section, away from the other periodicals. Finding consumer product information for our patrons is an important part of our job, especially now that so many people have begun doing their shopping on the Web.

Consumer Advice

Here are a few resources that can point our public in the right buying direction.

Consumer Reports Online
www.consumerreports.org

No, it's not free. Consumer Reports Online costs $19 annually if you subscribe to the print magazine. Otherwise, it's $26 for a year or $4.95 per month. Still, it's a terrific site, offering all the content of its print counterpart plus interactive tools for comparing products and an "e-Ratings: Web Site Review" page to help users find the best shopping sites on the Web.

ConsumerSearch
www.consumersearch.com

Derek Drew got tired of having to look in three different magazines to read all the reviews on one product. So, he started this site to pull consumer advice into one place. ConsumerSearch begins

Figure 9.1   Use ConsumerSearch to find reviews of reviews!

its process by reviewing the reviews about all different kinds of products, including those in *Consumer Reports*, listed previously. It looks for the best reviews, both on and off the Internet, and then ranks them according to how well they identify the category's best products. Next, it develops a "Full Story" report, identifying experts on these product categories and analyzing what they say. Finally, it distills the results about which products are top-rated into a "Fast Answers" section. This site covers big-ticket items—don't look for toaster reviews here.

Consumer Guide
www.consumerguide.com

My patrons consider this publication as the poor cousin of *Consumer Reports*. Still, Consumer Guide has gained reputation of late, particularly in the field of reviewing automobiles. The Web site offers this service for free, along with reviews of lots of other things consumers might fancy, including electronics and baby gear. The Consumer Guide site also features a price comparison engine with links to online merchants. Find the Mobil Travel Guide here, too, to help plan a trip and make reservations.

Hunter or Gatherer?

"There are two kinds of shoppers in the world," I once heard a comedian say, "Hunters and Gatherers." The Hunters, in true caveman fashion, walk into a store saying, "Me want shirt. Got shirt. Go home now." In contrast, the Gatherers get a basket and wander about, picking and choosing among brightly colored objects.

A confession: I am a Gatherer. As such, I actually find it relaxing to browse aimlessly, examine merchandise closely, and then reject it. I like to take a lot of time perusing specs and comparing prices, weighing all the factors before I buy. I drive my Hunter husband crazy. In contrast, Hunters know what they want and they don't want to mess around. For these shoppers, time saved is value added and worth any few cents they might save by comparing prices.

Shopping search engines offer a mix of product and merchant selection tools that gladden the heart of any Gatherer. A product selection feature allows users to compare similar products to decide which one to buy. Once the consumer has decided on a particular product, the merchant selection feature helps to find the best seller. Even if we don't use the engines to actually buy something, they can give us a strong overview of the products available and their price ranges.

Sites For Gatherers
Shopping Search Engines

Fellow Gatherers, here are some of the best general shopping search engines.

Shopping.com
www.shopping.com

This site has been around a long time in different identities. Recently, it was purchased by eBay.com. Shopping.com incorporates Epinions.com, and integrates their reviews of the products on sale. This is the best general shopping search engine, or "shop-bot," in that it offers a lot of information about every product and deals only with trustworthy merchants. Search for a known item or drill down through the directory structure to find an array of similar products.

BizRate.com
www.bizrate.com

BizRate searches for products, then ranks merchants according to its proprietary shopping search algorithm. Most of the input for merchant rank comes from millions of users who offer feedback about their shopping experiences each week. Keep track of your product and store reviews with a free BizRate account.

Yahoo! Shopping
http://shopping.yahoo.com

The Yahoo! shopping engine searches major chain stores as well as smaller merchants enrolled in its collection of online stores. Shop by store or by brand, or drill down into their directory structure of stuff for sale. Tip: visit the bottom of the splash page to link into free information from *Consumer Reports*.

PriceGrabber.com
www.pricegrabber.com

Wow! PriceGrabber.com not only searches for the lowest listed prices, but also figures in any taxes and shipping costs for the merchants, depending on where you order. Search here for books, consumer electronics, video games, movies, music, toys, and computers. Another perk of this site: no pop-up ads. Free registration makes users eligible for a tracking feature that will notify them of merchant price drops.

Froogle
http://froogle.google.com

Froogle is the shopping version of Google; that is, it applies Google's search technology to "locating stores that sell the item you want to find and pointing you directly to the place where you can make a purchase," according to the site. Froogle does not accept payment from merchants for higher ranking in the search results. Instead, demure targeted advertisements called "Sponsored Links" appear alongside the result list.

mySimon
www.mysimon.com

mySimon, now part of CNET, is quite a good comparison shopping service. The search results page allows users to sort merchants by price, availability of product, store name, and store rating. mySimon vets its merchants, so every seller in this database is considered trustworthy.

PriceSCAN.com
http://PriceSCAN.com

PriceSCAN is the "cleanest" of the shopping search engines in that it accepts no money from vendors for listing products and prices. In a product search, PriceSCAN will also search for "functionally equivalent products," finding the best prices among various manufacturers. Browse the store directory to find the online shopping site that best suits your needs. Here's a useful tip for those without prescription drug coverage: Type the name of a medication in the product search box. PriceSCAN will compare prices from pharmacies in the U.S. and Canada.

Ask Jeeves
www.ask.com

And you thought Jeeves was just a search engine. No way. Now, everyone's favorite butler serves up price comparisons, too. Simply click on the "Products" icon to bring up a cost comparison grid powered by PriceGrabber.com.

Specialized Shopping Search Engines

Just as it sometimes works best to use a subject-specific search engine when combing the Web, online shoppers can sometimes find a shopping search engine that specializes in the type of thing they want. These specialized shopping engines are much more likely to get relevant results. Here are some shopping search engines that specialize in particular categories of merchandise.

BookFinder.com
www.bookfinder.com

For finding the best prices on used books, you can't do better than BookFinder.com. Fast and efficient, BookFinder is the database to start with for used, fine, rare, and out-of-print books. It searches Advanced Book Exchange, Alibris, Amazon, Antiqbook, Bibliofind, Fatbrain, Powell's Books, and many others at once. That's a lot of books. Students use this site to find used textbooks. The service is run by Anirvan Chatterjee and his company, 13th Generation Media, based in Berkeley, California.

CNET Shopper
http://shopper.cnet.com

Buying computers, electronics, or wireless products? Go to CNET Shopper. This site also offers reviews of the latest gadgets. When a patron called wanting reviews of the latest cell phone, I found it here.

Mobissimo Travel
www.mobissimo.com/search_airfare.php

This newish metasearch travel engine operates on the same principle as the shopping search engines, but it searches for the best prices on airline tickets (outside of Southwest Airlines and jetBlue, who don't generally allow travel search engines to spider their databases). Mobissimo joins the ranks of older travel search engines including Cheap Tickets (www.cheaptickets.com), Expedia (www.expedia.com), Orbitz (www.orbitz.com), Travelocity (www.travelocity.com), Yahoo! Travel (http://travel.yahoo.com), and QIXO (www.qixo.com).

Figure 9.2   Find low rates on services such as loans and credit cards at LowerMyBills.com.

LowerMyBills.com
www.lowermybills.com

Let LowerMyBills.com help you find the lowest rates on services from loans to long distance to credit cards to Internet Service Providers.

GetConnected
www.getconnected.com

Enter your ZIP code to find local deals on wireless phones and plans, high-speed Internet access, long-distance phoning, and satellite television. When looking for cellular service, shop by phone, carrier, accessories, promotions, or "lifestyle."

Other Shopping Search Tools

eBay
www.ebay.com

I don't think any discussion of online shopping would be complete without mentioning that bastion on online auctions, eBay. I may window shop for new gear on the general shopping search engines. But if I really want a bargain, I will troll eBay for lightly used merchandise that suits my needs just fine. Even though sales usually happen between people and not corporations, most trans-actions are reasonably secure when paid through PayPal (www.paypal.com), eBay's banking auxiliary. Both buyers and sell-ers are rated on eBay by the feedback they receive on every trans-action. While eBay is not completely fraud free, the system usually works remarkably well, if you don't mind competing in an auction instead of just buying stuff.

SalesHound.com
www.saleshound.com

What local brick-and-mortar stores are having a sale? Use SalesHound.com to find deals that you can drive to. Sign up for e-mail alerts when the products you want go on sale at a chain store near you.

Sites for Hunters

Let's say that you don't want to mess around with finding the absolute lowest price for every darned thing that you are going to buy. You value convenience. You want to go to one site, click to buy what you want, and have it sent wherever you want it to go. You are a Hunter.

Never fear. Simply visit these sites to find your quarry quickly and have it dispatched post-haste.

Amazon
www.amazon.com

It's not just for books anymore. Amazon has teamed up with other quality merchants like Target to become a one-stop shop for dry goods, electronics, apparel, music, movies, tools, toys, gourmet food, kitchen appliances. (Sears Redux?) It is easy to use and very secure. You may never have to buy gifts at a physical store again.

Buy.com
www.buy.com

Find slightly dated electronics along with books, music, sporting goods, and toys for about the lowest price anywhere on the Web. There are lots of selections here to keep a Hunter happy on the first foray.

Outpost.com
www.outpost.com

In California, we have a whimsical discount computer chain called Fry's Electronics. Every brick-and-mortar manifestation of this company has a unique decorative scheme. At my local branch in Burbank, aliens have crashed their spaceship above the entrance to the store. Inside, they hover from the rafters as mannequin commandos take aim at them from among the merchandise. This company's online presence, Outpost.com, is not so pixilated. Still, it offers some pretty great deals on all kinds of consumer electronics and household appliances.

E-Coupons

In the spirit of saving money by shopping on the Web, let's pick up some online coupons before we start. These coupon listings have the added benefit of suggesting specific online merchants that we may want to visit.

CoolSavings.com
www.coolsavings.com

Sign up to print out savings coupons for products sold at brick-and-mortar stores.

AbleShoppers.com
www.ableshoppers.com

AbleShoppers scours the Web for things on sale. It also lists electronic coupons usable at online stores. Pick up its RSS feed to keep on top of those bargains.

eCoupons
www.ecoupons.com

Here is a kind of electronic coupon and sale search engine. Browse categories of merchants, for example, apparel, books, and computers, or zip down the alpha list of stores. This list links to dealers offering either merchandise on sale or electronic discount codes for use at checkout. More than 160 quality sellers are represented here, from Amazon to Nordstrom to Wal-Mart.

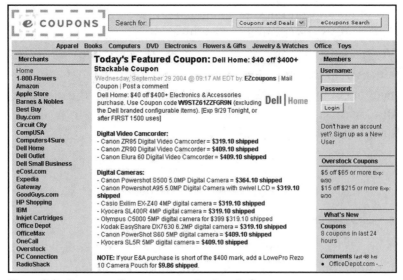

Figure 9.3   Browse online coupons and sales at eCoupons.com.

SmartSource: Grocery Coupons
http://coupons.smartsource.com

The company that brings us weekly coupon savings in our Sunday newspaper and stocks our stores with little red coupon dispensing machines now offers online coupons for printing on our computers, via a special downloadable "coupon print manager" program. This authenticity is important because coupons are a form of money: Retailers cannot honor copied versions because they don't get their money back from the product makers. Note:

SmartSource is a marketing company. I wouldn't be surprised if the "coupon print manager" also sends some feedback to SmartSource every time a user chooses a coupon. That's why the service is "free," I suppose.

FatWallet
www.fatwallet.com

It's a coupon site. No, it's a shopping search engine. Wait! You're both right. Complete the free registration to link to sales at online merchants or to participate in the feedback "Forums." Use the "Compare Prices" page to access cost comparison content provided by PriceGrabber.com. The latest spin? On this site, getting a rebate is reframed as earning "Cash Back." Only you don't actually get the money. It stays in your FatWallet account as credit against future purchases.

E-Commerce and Security

When I teach Internet classes at the library and talk about buying things over the Web, my students invariably ask me, "Is it safe?"

As with so many things about the Internet, the answer is complicated.

Generally, yes, it is safe to use a credit card over the Web to buy from well-known companies that use "secure" technology, that is, they encrypt your credit card number and other personal information as it is transmitted over the Web. Here is a site that explains how merchants can keep their purchasers safe.

Learn the Net: Security
www.learnthenet.com/english/html/07secur.htm

This site explains how credit card transactions over the Web are scrambled so that hackers can't intercept them. It also lists the signs that buyers are dealing with reputable merchants—and where to complain if they are not.

Great, I feel safer already. Still, we have all read about thefts of credit card data that have occurred recently. These were not card numbers that were stolen as they crossed the Internet. This data were stolen from information brokers, companies whose only business is to store that information securely: ChoicePoint, in Alpharetta, Georgia, and Tucson, Arizona-based CardSystems Solutions. There are other loose links in the system. Recently, the United Parcel Service lost data tapes that it was transporting for Citigroup. The tapes contained personal financial information for nearly four million people.

The CardSystems theft compromised the privacy of some 40 million credit card accounts. Yet there are billions of credit cards issued worldwide. So in order of magnitude, 40 million is actually not that many, considering how many accounts are out there.

Still, should we consumers be concerned? Yes, especially when these companies do not disclose breaches in their security. In California, there is now a law that requires that customers be notified when their data has been stolen. There, at least, people will know when their data has been hacked.

Eugene H. Spafford, executive director of the Center for Education and Research in Information Assurance and Security at Purdue University, has noted that if security breaches increase, the federal government may have to step in. Still, that may not completely solve the problem of electronic information theft.

In all my Web-based shopping, I feel fortunate never to have suffered credit card theft. On the other hand, as I tell my classes, one Thursday, I returned a $2.97 terra cotta pot to Home Depot. On Saturday, I received a call at home asking me if I was trying to use my card at a Texaco station. Apparently, a clerk had passed on my number to a credit card fraud ring, which got busy right away trying to use it.

And that had nothing to do with the Internet.

All Shopped Out

Whew! I hope you found what you were hunting for, no matter what your shopping style. I know that I certainly have. Now all I need to find is a service to shovel all the stuff that I have bought out of my house so I can make room for more!

Part 2

The Librarian as Information Technician: Working with the Medium and the Machines

While weeding the (Dewey) 600s recently, I came across a facsimile edition of a 1927 Sears and Roebuck catalog. On one page appeared the offer for a mechanized, oil-saving, hog greaser.

Has someone been using this device on information technology? Because sometimes it seems to librarians that mastering the protean nature of computer technology is like trying to catch a greased hog. Just when we think we've finally got it, it mutates, slips through our arms, and keeps on running.

Of course, we want to help our patrons find information. But before we can do that, we have to spend time wrestling with the beast. Hence, this last section of the book, which will cover some of the skills we must learn to adapt our craft to the Internet and the computers on which it runs. If we can just master a few new tricks, we will see how doing reference on the Web is not so different from doing it in print. The Internet can become just an additional tool at our disposal, albeit a large slippery one with a mind of its own.

Chapter 10

Managing Web-Based E-Mail

It was about 2001 when I first saw someone use wireless e-mail. I was sitting in a training session for a new system that was, frankly, not yet ready for prime time. The ditzy trainer seemed more interested in describing his recent trip to Las Vegas than his company's glitchy product. There I sat—a librarian trapped in an all-day training from hell. As I fidgeted and twisted in my chair, I noticed the guy across the aisle. He was calm. He had a slight smile on his face. He was concentrating on the tiny cell phone in his hand. Tap, tap, he went with a plastic stylus. What was he doing? Oh my gosh, he was reading his e-mail!

At that moment, desire for that link to the outside world overwhelmed me. I would have paid dearly to be able to write e-mail from a dumb little cell phone. Today, my jealousy has been assuaged and for little cost. I can do e-mail and text messaging, a kind of "e-mail lite," on the cell phone that I got for free with my wireless plan.

It's not just librarians who love e-mail so much. These days, businesspeople shell out the bucks for wireless e-mail devices such as RIM's BlackBerry (www.blackberry.com). Wireless e-mail allows us restless go-getters to feel that we can do two things at once. "Internet executives rave about watching messages roll in while they conduct other business," wrote Amy Harmon in the *New York Times* ("E-Mail You Can't Outrun," September 21, 2000).

This trend caused one vice president of a major investment bank to complain, "You go to meetings and it's hard to get those guys to focus because they're all pecking away." "Staff meetings are not worth holding if everybody is there thumb-typing," gripes the chief executive of a Northern California Internet company.

Some professionals are so obsessed that they fiddle with their e-mail when they should attend to their spouses. One lawyer remarked, "I've heard colleagues say that when they've had the poor taste to return e-mails from their bedrooms, it hasn't been a welcome gesture."

Goodness gracious! Well, it seems that neither librarians nor business professionals can live without e-mail. How about everyone else? A survey from the USC Annenberg Center for the Digital Future reveals that, in the year 2004, a decade after the birth of the graphical Web, "The Internet is used by about three-quarters of Americans, and online technology is a constant presence in two-thirds of American homes" (www.digitalcenter.org). E-mail is still the single most important reason people go online, according to the survey. Indeed, it is determined that 70.2 percent of Americans now use e-mail.

To understand the importance of e-mail, we must look back at the history of the Internet. It is 1970. ARPANET has been established by the U.S. military to send important files in distributed fashion between supercomputers. On these top-secret files rests the security of the nation. Along with these files come messages: "Sgt. Rumbolt, run this program at oh-eight-hundred hours. Oh, and BTW, how are your kids?"

Fast forward to 1980: The ARPANET has been opened to the academic community and is now known as the Internet. Professor X uses it to send a message to Professor Y: "Here is my latest theorem. What do you think? BTW, how are your kids?"

A quarter of a century later, in the public library, a harried soccer mom brings her family in for a little after-dinner homework session. She snatches a much-needed break at the library's Internet terminals and writes her sister, "Jane, are we on for Thanksgiving? BTW, how are the kids?"

I Want My E-Mail

Throughout the 30-something years that the Internet (by whatever name) has existed, e-mail has remained its most popular protocol, the tried-and-true "killer app." It dovetails with the basic human need to communicate. E-mail is easy, asynchronous, and inexpensive. Usually, Internet access accounts that come with e-mail charge a monthly fee, although Web-based e-mail accounts such as those on MSN's Hotmail (www.hotmail.com) are free. That makes it the medium of choice for many folks to send messages around the country and the world. Contact one friend or colleague at a time—or many. You don't have the time to call each one? Send out a broadcast message.

E-mail lacks the "tone of voice" of spoken communication, but this is not always a bad thing. I know one fellow who reconciled with his father using e-mail. He couldn't stand the sarcastic timbre of his dad's voice over the phone. But e-mail gave them both the space to use cool heads in their communication and free their messages from insinuation.

E-mail is *quiet*, which makes it a perfect communication protocol for a library. If there is one thing that yanks my chain, it is the tinny tune of a cell phone ring, followed by the yammering of a patron who apparently thinks that the reference area is a private phone booth. How much better for everyone if these folks conducted their conversations via touch-typing!

Also, most commercial services expect users to have an e-mail address. For example, you must have an e-mail account to buy an airline ticket online because that is where they send your electronic confirmation.

For all these reasons, if your library offers Internet access to your patrons, you must also give them e-mail. Of course. Why wouldn't you? There are several reasons, rooted in the history of the Internet again.

At first, all e-mail came via the telnet protocol. In this protocol, your machine acted as a remote console for the big computer that stored your messages. Although you could read your mail on the screen, it never stayed on your local hard drive unless you specifically downloaded it. This kept your hard drive free of extraneous files.

The mid-1990s saw the creation of POP3 mail (Post Office Protocol), in which a program on your machine, for example Eudora (www.eudora.com), opens a connection to your ISP, downloads your mail, then cuts the connection. You reconnect when you are ready to send. With most e-mail work done offline, the time spent hogging a live connection to the Internet drops dramatically. The problem for public access terminals? Users must reconfigure the e-mail program whenever they access a different account. Plus, users' private e-mail downloads to the public terminal—a total drag for everyone concerned!

Then came Web-based e-mail, which some outfits gave away "free," for the price of a small advertisement attached to all messages. Hotmail, acquired by Microsoft, makes one's e-mail account accessible from any Internet terminal, eliminates the need for middleman software, and solves the e-mail dilemma for public access terminals. When the Internet was riding high in the late 1990s, many commercial Web sites offered free e-mail accounts in order to attract repeat visitors. Although many of these accounts disappeared after the "dot-gone" bust, good, free, Web-based e-mail service is still widely available.

Everyone lives happily ever after. Well, almost. There remains the possibility that a patron could download a virus through the mail and open it on your hard drive. But that could happen through any access to the open Web, not just e-mail. Your best protection is strong, regularly updated anti-virus software, such as Symantec's Norton Anti-Virus (www.symantec.com/index.htm), or VirusScan from McAfee (www.mcafee.com/us).

If you follow these precautions, you will have immense success in offering free, Web-based e-mail to your patrons. But, as always, with tremendous triumph comes other problems—like trying to pry obsessive-compulsives off your public terminals when their time is up, for example. Still, this is a happy problem, a sign that you are doing something right.

When you get your public Internet access system in place and things flow well, then magic happens. Standing by our public access terminals the other day, I realized that I had one patron typing e-mail in French, another in Spanish, one in German, and two more in Chinese. "Wow," I thought, "this is what the World Wide Web is all about."

Free E-Mail Directories

Your patrons want and need free e-mail. You and your staff may need it, too, depending on the state of Internet access for your library. I talked to a colleague who complained that her library had only one e-mail account for the whole reference department. What? Why? We librarians need to have a way to communicate with our patrons and each other.

Here are some directories and lists to help you find a free e-mail service just right for your patrons—or for you.

Free E-mail Providers Guide: FEPG.net
www.fepg.net

Cole and Associates brings you the Free E-mail Providers Guide, featuring 1,300 free e-mail providers from around the world. Let "Posty" the e-mail wizard help you decide which free e-mail service would work best for you. FEPG.net keeps us up-to-date with the free e-mail universe, offering news on its site or pushing the news to your (free) e-mail inbox.

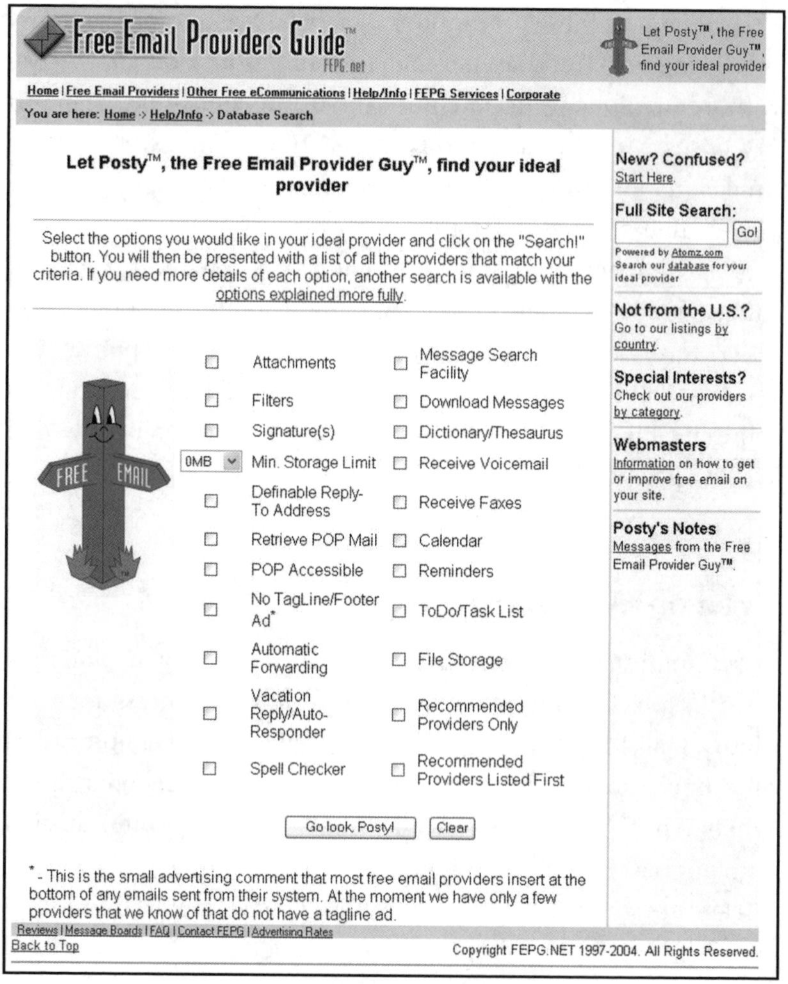

Figure 10.1 Let "Posty" the e-mail wizard help you decide which free e-mail
service would work best for you.

Yahoo! List of Free E-Mail
http://dir.yahoo.com

From the Yahoo! directory, search for "free e-mail." Then browse
Yahoo!'s hand-picked list of tasty free e-mail services. Short annotations help guide you to a site that will fill your needs.

Quality Free E-Mail

Here are a few sites that offer outstanding free e-mail services.

Yahoo! Mail
http://mail.yahoo.com

Everyone likes this full-featured e-mail service. It is integrated with other free Yahoo! features such as its "Briefcase" storage space, instant messaging service, and its RSS aggregator My Yahoo (http://my.yahoo.com). Plus, Yahoo! Mail offers 100 MB of mailbox capacity.

Hotmail
www.hotmail.com

A Microsoft product, this granddaddy of all free Web-based e-mail providers has increased its mailbox capacity to 250 megabytes, up from two megabytes. Beware, though. Hotmail accounts are often prime spammer targets. Also, these accounts become inactive if unused for 30 days. Ninety days of inactivity cause them to disappear altogether.

E-mailAnywhere.com
www.e-mailanywhere.com

The Canadian corporation MPC Technologies powers this Web page that gives users access to their e-mail from anywhere on the Web. The company also has a nice free e-mail service. I use this service as my "spam-bait" address when I sign up for contests and such.

Spymac
www.spymac.com/index.php

This Web-based e-mail service is designed for Mac users, although PC users can use it, too. It offers one gigabyte of storage for free. Plus, you can mount a Web page and post your photos.

Mail2Web
www.mail2web.com

You are on the road and can't dial into your ISP? Point your browser to Mail2Web to check any POP3 e-mail account not hidden behind a firewall.

GMail

http://mail.google.com/mail

In the spring of 2004, the famed search engine Google announced a new free e-mail service called GMail. GMail offers 2,000 megabytes, that is, two gigabytes, of e-mail storage. What's the catch? GMail serves up targeted advertising along with your messages. How do they know what ads to show? By electronically scanning your messages, that's how.

Of course, all e-mail services worth using scan messages to keep out spam and viruses. Also, the kind of subtle, relevant advertising such as that shown on Google is much better than blinking banners bearing spyware.

One can do a lot with a gigabyte of Web storage space. Users could store PowerPoint presentations or large digital photographs or backup data from their own computers for access from anywhere on the Web.

GMail is an amazing product that can serve many uses. Still, I wouldn't use my GMail account to send messages that mention anything I want kept private, such as medical conditions or affairs of the heart, if you receive my meaning. Hackers and terrorists would be advised to go elsewhere for free e-mail, too. However, if you have colleagues, friends, and coworkers you really trust, enough to share a single password account, it could also make a wonderful free collaborating tool. Perhaps the best effect of GMail's tremendous capacity? It has caused rival Yahoo! Mail and Hotmail to increase their free storage offerings, too.

Choosing a Screen Name

Part of the fun—and challenge—of choosing a free e-mail service lies in finding a login or screen name. Popular e-mail services have millions of subscribers—at the end of 2003, AOL alone had 24.3 million—and one of them almost certainly shares the name you want, no matter how unusual. Imagine trying to explain to your Internet-challenged patrons: "No, I'm sorry, Mrs. Krzyzanowski, your screen name is already taken. Perhaps you would like to call yourself 'PKrzyzanowski1234'?"

You can see the dilemma. After all, your screen name is your online identity. Joseph Janes, founding director of the Internet Public Library, has noted that his librarians tended to stereotype Internet patrons based on screen and domain names, just as we all assess patrons based on appearance in face-to-face interactions. For example, AOL users are sometimes viewed as less Internet-savvy than others. So, it makes a difference what you call yourself—and even which Internet Service Provider you choose.

Dr. Steven Jones, a communications professor at the University of Illinois in Chicago, has observed that people choose personal e-mail names according to what he calls the "concert T-shirt effect." That is, they tend to adopt the name of something they like, such as a band or a fairy-tale character. For chat rooms and messaging services, people will pick names to match the personalities they wish to project. "Just like adolescents," Jones notes. "Because we have a high degree of anonymity on e-mail, the screen name is the only thing that distinguishes us" ("Good Screen Names Are Hard to Find and Getting Harder," Joyce Cohen, *New York Times*, September 7, 2000).

Because your screen name is your main online identity, you might want to steer clear of the big free services such as Hotmail, Yahoo! Mail, and AOL. Try a newer domain or one associated with your interests. That way, if you ever have to give your e-mail on a resume, your future boss won't be writing to you to set up a job interview at the e-mail address BabyDoll or HotSexyMan@excite. com. On the other hand, if your handle is too common, you may become the target of misdirected mail. For example, when I was "irene@netcom.com," I got notes from all over the world. Sorry everyone! Good night, Irene!

Account Information	*Your e-mail address is your Web identity*
E-mail Address	FoxyLady123 @hotmail.com
Password Six-character minimum; no spaces	●●●●●● *Type zero for "o" and number 1 for "i"*
Retype Password	●●●●●● *e.g. "na1lp0l1sh"*
Secret Question	Favorite pet's name?
Secret Answer	Fluffy
Alternate E-mail Address (Optional)	
	Password-reset instructions are sent to this account. More...
Registration Check	Type the characters that you see in this picture. Why?
	BC262NGG
	I can't see this picture.
	BC262NGG
	Characters are not case-sensitive.

Figure 10.2   Choose your login name carefully.

How to choose a password? I advise choosing a word that describes something that you like and can remember, for instance "football." Then, substitute zeroes for the Os, and ones for the letters "L" or "I." Is there an "E" in the word? Substitute the number "3", which looks kind of like the letter "E" backwards. Since passwords are case sensitive, make the whole thing lowercase except for some odd letter in the middle. The result will be pretty darned unguessable, yet memorable to you: *f00tBal1*, for example. Once you find a good password, you can pretty well use it for all your free e-mail accounts, or, if you're very security minded, you might want to come up with different ones.

Attach This

One of the "pleasures" of offering public e-mail access in the library is that we not only have to help folks set up their accounts, but we get to show them how to use them, too. I constantly have patrons asking how to download or upload an attachment. An attachment is a file sent along with an e-mail message. It can be any kind: digital pictures, a word-processing file, a program, even a virus. Attached files retain all of their properties despite being sent through the mail. Because attachments can harbor harmful software, it is risky to open them.

Viruses often appear as attachments disguised as harmless information. One double click on that attached file opens a Pandora's Box of untold evils onto the hard drive. Consequently, we should all be paranoid about opening any e-mail attachment, at least until we have checked it out with our aforementioned ultra-up-to-date anti-virus program.

What if a patron—a student, say—wants to send a paper to a professor as an e-mail attachment? Have the student access his or her Web e-mail account and begin to compose a message. Somewhere on that composition page will appear a button with the word "attach" or some variation of it, indicating the system expects a filename. Click on that button, then make the computer browse to the "A:" drive, to the floppy disk on which the student has stored the paper. Click to choose the document, then click on the attach button on this page, which should send you back to the composition screen. Press "Send," and off goes the paper, ready for decoding by the professor at the other end. Cool!

Note that the student's paper must be written with the same software that the professor will use to read it. For example, I had a patron who was having no luck sending his resume to potential employers. Why? He wrote the document using WordPerfect from Corel (www.corel.com). The recipients were using an incompatible program, Microsoft Word (http://office.microsoft.com), to do word processing. Fortunately, I could convert his WordPerfect document into the Microsoft Word format, making it easy for potential employers to read his resume. The MS Word software also comes

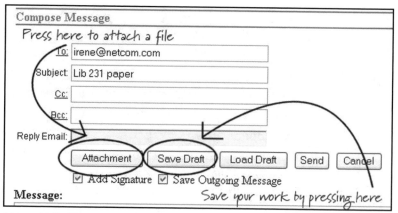

Figure 10.3   You can attach files to Web-based e-mail.

with a conversion program that works on WordPerfect documents. The sender could have written an e-mail message to alert the recipient to possible conversion problems. But somehow expecting a potential employer to have to do software tweaking to read your resume probably doesn't set the right tone for a job seeker. One way or another, the sender and the recipients must own the same software or an appropriate conversion program to read a document or view an image sent as an attachment.

If you have a timer on your public access machines, you will want to teach your patrons how to save a draft of their e-mails. Nothing irritates users more than spending 45 minutes composing the perfect message to the folks back home only to have it disappear when they run out of time. Most Web-based e-mail applications have a "save drafts" function. As long as users save drafts as they write, they can log back in and resume the message where they left off, even if the machine turns off before they got a chance to send. If your public access machines allow users to provide their own floppy disks, they might also save their evolving e-mails to the "A:" drive.

Spam Management

Spam is any electronic message mass-mailed on the Internet that forces itself on people who would not otherwise choose to receive it. The technical term for it is "Unsolicited Commercial E-mail" or "UCE." You know what I'm talking about: those sordid, pandering messages that clog our inboxes every day. "The spam messages I've seen have almost without exception advertised stuff that's worthless, deceptive, and partly or entirely fraudulent," states John Levine, co-author of *The Internet for Dummies*. "It's funky miracle cures, vaguely described get-rich-quick schemes, dial-a-porn, and so on downhill from there. It's all stuff that's too cruddy to be worth advertising in any medium where they'd actually have to pay the cost of the ads" (http://spam.abuse.net/overview/spambad.html).

Spam has become a major nuisance. In April 2005, *Scientific American* reported that two-thirds of worldwide e-mail consisted of unwanted commercial solicitations. For some users, 80 percent of the messages that they receive are spam (Goodman, J., et al. "Stopping Spam." *Scientific American*, 292:4, April 2005, p. 42). System administrators must deal with the bombardment of Internet messages that clog their servers and threaten their networks with malicious programs. End-users plow through piles of offensive junk to pick out the few notes they need from work and family. It is getting to the point at which e-mail interferes with productivity rather than promotes it.

Can't we pass a law that stops spam? We tried. The "CAN-SPAM Act of 2003" went into effect the following year. Unfortunately, most spam is written within the U.S., but *sent* from servers located outside the boundaries of the U.S., where federal law has no power.

It is almost impossible to stop spam at its source. If we respond to spam, asking to be removed from their mailing list, say, the spammers slam back with even more unsolicited mail. Our best hope of managing spam is to use software designed to filter out these messages before we ever see them.

Reputable ISPs filter most obvious spam for their users. Free Web-based e-mail accounts often come equipped with "anti-spam" filters. When users receive unwanted messages, the filters enable them to add the sender to a blocked list. After that, any more communication from that sender gets deleted before it reaches the inbox.

Are spam filters perfect? Oh no. For one thing, spammers change their address of origin all the time to get around the filters. Still, if used diligently, anti-spam software can go a long way to reducing the amount of spam in our inboxes to a manageable level.

It had better. Otherwise, e-mail will become more trouble than it is worth.

Getting Off Commercial E-mail Lists
www.dmaconsumers.org/consumers/optoutform_
emps.shtml

Want to reduce the amount of unsolicited e-mail, a.k.a. spam, that floods your inbox? Sign up with the Direct Marketing Association's "E-mail Preference Service." Legitimate companies will check this list and remove your name from their mailing lists. Of course, nasty ones with no ethics will continue to send you junk. Still, signing up here may cut down on the volume. A free sign-up buys one year of protection.

MailWasher
www.mailwasher.net

To avoid spam, I don't reveal my work e-mail address to marketers. Needless to say, I was surprised the other day to see pictures of naked gals in inviting (?) postures in my inbox beneath come-hither text written in—Korean! Oh come on! It was time to download Nick Bolton's freeware program that allows Windows users to preprocess their POP3 e-mail. This lets you view the subject lines of incoming messages to decide whether to bring them on down or delete and bounce. The bounced e-mails are returned to sender with a note saying that the address no longer exists. MailWasher also recognizes and warns users of possible spam and will automatically block messages from user-specified senders. It can even filter according to character sets, that is, by language. If you like the program, send Nick some money.

Thunderbird
www.mozilla.org/products/thunderbird

This free e-mail program for PCs allows users to identify spam with a click of the mouse. Future messages from identified spammers get shunted to the "junk" folder or to the trash. The application is easy to use and very effective.

What About Chat?

Chat and instant messaging (IM) can be very cool for connecting with friends. Unlike e-mail, these formats transmit messages in real time. But chat and IM usually require the user to download secondary software, definitely a problem for public access terminals. Chat and IM software must be configured for every account, just as the old e-mail software used to be. Once users have logged in, the software remembers and reactivates whenever someone attempts to contact them.

Imagine this scene: Although "HeatherS" logged off hours ago, her friends still try to reach her. Because she has downloaded chat software onto your public access hard drive, the middle-aged patron checking his stock prices after work suddenly gets interrupted by a chat window. "Hey Heather. Want to go to the mall? Heather?" It is now up to you, a reference librarian, to apologize to the stock checker, kick him off the computer, then get into that machine, and remove the chat program as fast as you can. Good luck.

The two major IM programs, AOL Instant Messenger (www.aim.com) and ICQ (ICQ stands for "I Seek You"; www.icq.com) also owned by America Online, require those insidious downloads. Still, there are a few chat and IM services entirely Java based; they need no extra software beyond a late model browser to run. Give them a try.

Yahoo! Chat
http://chat.yahoo.com

Although Yahoo! does offer pernicious downloadable chat room software, it also sponsors these more modern java-based chat rooms that leave no trace on library computers.

InfiniteChat
www.infinitechat.com

Here are several rooms for teens, kids, adults, and trivia lovers. All are free and require no registration or plug-ins, as they are Java-based. Just choose a nickname and jump right in.

Headbone Zone Chat
www.headbone.com/friends/chat

How about a nice, safe place for kids to chat under the watchful eye of a grown-up? Here it is. Kids and teens just need to sign up, read and agree to the rules (no personal information, no objectionable language, etc.), then begin chatting. The chat rooms are only open when an adult is monitoring them.

Notice that I haven't addressed the *worthiness* of chat. Our library has only six public access Internet computers. Call us controlling, sure. Still, we would prefer to keep these few precious resources available for research or sending notes to loved ones across the world. On the other hand, if people sign up and wait like everyone else, why should it concern us if some patrons use our machines for pleasure instead of work?

This issue is one that time and cheaper, improved technology will resolve. When we move to wireless Internet access, patrons can use their own machines to do whatever they wish on the Web.

This opens us up to liability issues if they use our Web for illegal activities. Still, we face that problem on our machines now. We all need a solid Internet access policy to protect us in case of illegal patron use, for example, making terrorist threats or downloading child pornography.

The teens who like to chat are way ahead of us librarians, anyway. They don't really need us. Heck, they can simply pull out their cell phones and thumb type chat to each other. (The joints in my middle-age thumbs start to throb at the *thought* of that.) They can send still photos, too, and even upload them to their mobile phone blogs, or "moblogs." Kids today.

Mr. Post Ma-a-an

Now that you know all, there is no excuse for you or your users to live without electronic communication anytime, anywhere there is a computer attached to the Internet. Of course, you must remind your users—and remember yourself—that e-mail is one of the least private methods of communication. The format invites confession and retransmission (aka forwarding). One wise rule of thumb: Never send anything in an e-mail message that you would regret seeing on the front page of tomorrow's newspaper.

Most information professionals I know have at least three e-mail accounts: one for work, one for home, and a junk one to feed to "free" registration sites. If one goes down, the other two are sure to work. Now comes the new problem: how to tell which of those dozens of e-mails coming in every day are important enough to read!

Chapter 11

Tips for Teaching the Internet

I became a librarian for many reasons, but there is one thing I am sure of: I did not study Information Science for two years so that I could become a teacher. My husband teaches. I am an expert information finder, reluctant to share my hard-won techniques with anyone.

Yet all reference librarians these days, whether working in corporate offices or inner city branches, eventually find themselves with the responsibility of training their clients in how to use the Web. It's cool, it's convenient, and they're going to try to use it no matter what you do. They'll just waste hours trying to find something when they could have asked you and you could have pulled it up in a minute. It is so satisfying to play the role of magician, *n'est-ce pas*? Still, it gets to be a drag when, after a while, your clients come to think that you, and only you, can solve their information quandaries—especially when they want you to solve them 24/7. Additionally, questions about the Internet have a nasty way of sliding into technical support issues, with questions such as, "How do I straighten my text columns?" emerging after your patron "tap-tap-tapped" the space bar instead of using the formatting features of Microsoft Word when making columns.

Really, we should give our patrons some clues as to how to do simple Web searches themselves. Teaching, however, is an entirely different skill from finding—a professional searcher's primary area of expertise. Our patrons have little use for the minutiae we find so fascinating—like the relative merits of various search engines, for example. It's back to basics. But how can we teach the basics without putting our clients—and ourselves—to sleep?

The "Beginner Mind"

One of the most important things a trainer can do is to recapture the "beginner mind," that is, to try to remember what it was like before they knew anything about online searching or the Internet. As Mary Ellen Mort, creator of JobStar (www.jobstar.org), has said, "No matter how smart we get, we value remembering what it felt like to be stupid. It is our link to the user" (Talk given at the Southern California Online Users Group (SCOUG) Spring Workshop, 1997).

When she thinks about training, Mary Ellen likes to visualize trying to teach the Internet to her Uncle Louie. Oh no! Not Uncle Louie!

Cindy A. Gruwell, assistant librarian and coordinator of User Instruction at the University of Minnesota Biomedical Library, concurs. "You absolutely can't take for granted that your user is computer literate! This extends beyond the realm of databases. I think that we tend to treat the young folk as if they are born with keyboards at their fingertips. This is not true—and is, in fact, a disservice to all users. Everyone is an individual, and people's expertise runs the range from novice to wizard" (From a private e-mail; reprinted with permission). That goes, not only for Uncle Louie, but also for a CEO or city councilperson who wants private Internet searching lessons.

Your students will cover a wide gamut in terms of their Web and basic computer knowledge. Some may know how to point and click and get to their Hotmail, while others may not know how to type or maneuver a mouse. Unfortunately, you have to teach to the lowest common denominator. Assess the students as soon as they come into your class, so you'll know where to set your level.

How do you do that? One technique involves passing out index cards to your students as they enter. Ask them to write the answer to the question, "What do you want to get out of this class?" Collect the cards and review them before you begin. Structure your training based on the answers on the cards.

Active Learning

Oh, how I love "active learning," which is broadly understood to mean that students spend most of the class time taking tools into their own hands and learning by doing. This means that you, the instructor, are relieved of the burden of single-handedly keeping a roomful of strangers entertained for an hour. You just give them a little overview, break them up into small groups, hand out assignments, and then hang around coaching for the rest of the class period, giving little tips here and some pointers there. At the end of class, you force your students to stand up and report their findings. Voilà. The class is over, and the students have done all the work.

You can even compel them to cement their knowledge by asking them to write a "one-minute paper" on the topic, "What did you learn?" and "What do you still want to know?" You can ask them to report on that, too.

When you separate your class into little working groups, be sure to pair the more advanced students with the absolute beginners. This has a double advantage: The experienced students don't get so bored when they have partners to help, and they end up doing the drudge work, not you.

Yes, active learning is a great technique, both for indolent instructors (like me), and for students. They take responsibility for learning, and the teacher takes the credit.

The Part Where You Talk

First of all, never—and I mean never—try to cram too much into one session. Pick out three main points that you want to get across, just three, and leave it at that. Even Einstein couldn't remember more than that, not to mention Uncle Louie. You can't cover everything in one session, so don't even try. Pick three topics and cover them well.

When I teach beginners, I like to sketch a conceptual overview of the Internet, rather than plodding through a procedural how-to. I sense that students need some kind of a mental model of the Web. I quiz them about their knowledge. What is the Internet? How old is it? Who runs it? If there is pornography on the Web, why can't we make laws to stop it? Why are search engines free? Who can put things on the Web? How?

Analogies are a great way to help neophytes land right side up in cyberspace. Yahoo! works like a phone book. Think of bookmarks as speed dialing. When you use TCP/IP to cross the Internet, it's like Captain Kirk demanding, "Beam me up, Scotty!" on Star Trek. Your e-mail breaks up into a million pieces, disappears, and then reassembles at its destination, just like the captain and crew of the Starship Enterprise.

"Teach time economy!" declares Internet trainer Sara Weissman ("Shoptalk," *NetConnect*, supplement to *Library Journal*, April 16, 2000). "Three search engines or 20 minutes with no hits means it's time to rethink the search or call the library!"

Weissman suggests teaching Web address structure: .com is commercial, .org is nonprofit, .gov is government, and .edu is academe. She guarantees that your class will be surprised that they can often guess Internet addresses. All it takes is thinking about who put the information on the Web in the first place—and why. I call that "Follow the money." This is the essence of critical thinking, the key to separating the gems from the junk on the Internet.

Searching the Web is a lot like shopping at an off-price store. You have to pick through a lot of cheap rayon rejects to find the occasional Jones New York silk jacket for $27 in the right size (which I did not too long ago at a Macy's outlet). There's that critical-thinking element coming in again. How do you feel, taste, smell a Web page to judge its worth?

I make a handout for my classes listing Web quality points. These are essentially the same checkpoints that librarians use when doing collection development. The first point I talk about is "Authority": Who wrote the page? What credentials does the writer have to be an authority on the subject? I teach students that every page should be signed by its author and should offer an e-mail link to that person.

The second point is "Currency." Remember that the Web only really took off in 1995; any page not updated in the last six months is history. Make sure the page is dated and recent.

Point three is "Accuracy or Bias." It costs money to rent server space for a Web page. Follow that money. Who put up that page and why? I tell the story of looking up abortion statistics for a student at the University of Southern California. We found some instantly, with the caveat that the figures for the last three years were "estimated." Who paid the rent on that page? The Ohio Right to Life League. Biased? You decide. On the other hand, the Web is a great place to find biased information that the library would never spend money to collect. The Internet offers a platform to wackos of all political persuasions. Just be sure to recognize them as such.

"Commercialism" is my fourth quality checkpoint. A site that sells things is terrific, if you want to buy something, like an off-price jacket from REI Outlet (www.rei.com/outlet/index.html) or an airplane ticket. But if you only want information, beware. It may well lie elsewhere on the Web, or at the library, for free. Scholarship and health information are areas particularly prone to fraud. Remember that the only two types of resources that have so far succeeded with charging for access are sites that give financial advice (people will gladly pay money to make more money) and pornographic services. Both, I guess, fulfill some basic human drives.

Some trainers combine the previous two points into "Purpose": Why is someone paying the rent on that Web page? Is it to teach, persuade, or sell? When your students automatically consider the source and purpose of the information they find, they are well equipped to safely sail the rocky seas of the open Web.

My final consideration is "Scope": Does the information on the Web answer your question, and in enough depth? Health information on the Web will help you understand your condition in general, but only your doctor can tell you what is right for your particular case. Often, the Web works best at identifying the expert in the field and supplying contact information, you can talk to that person yourself. It empowers you by giving you enough information so that you can become an active partner with professionals in solving your problems. It helps you learn what questions to ask. Like a liberal arts education, the Web helps you to know what you don't know, that is, to get a sense of the issues in a subject area, even if you aren't an expert.

These critical-thinking skills are essential for Internet students at every level. As Mary Ellen Mort says, "Life is ambiguous. We must teach patrons how to make decisions when the facts aren't clear."

The Part Where They Work

Now, it's your students' turn. After you divide them up into groups of two or three, give them index cards and have them write down something that they want to find on the Web. Then, have them trade cards with the others in their group. Now, ask them to find results for their neighbor's question. Students seem to really enjoy solving other people's problems. Also, this keeps the groups engaged, chatting about the progress of their mutual searches.

Ask your students to evaluate the information they have found using the checklist of quality points listed above. Choose someone in each group to "sell" a chosen site to the rest of the class based on these points.

What if you do not have a computer training room? What if the class is too large for hands-on training? You can use one computer to show your trainees Web resources that suit their subject needs. If your group has no specific needs, or if the needs vary widely, do your demonstration with a search about a controversial topic that has hit the news in the last three days. That way, the whole class will be interested and working from the same frame of reference.

After your demonstration, you might try playing "Good Site/Bad Site," in which you ask the class to evaluate particular sites based on the quality checklist. Or you might use a quiz-show model, dividing your students into teams. Offer them a list of sites and ask them, "Which source would you use?" The first team to choose the correct resource wins. I give my teams squeaky toys or bicycle bells so they can "ring in" when they get the answer. All these goings-on can get very silly, yet it certainly does keep the students active and involved.

Can you teach people to use the Internet if you have no computer access at all? Yes, said Patricia Iannuzzi, Dean of University Libraries at the University of Nevada, Las Vegas, at a 1994 American Library Association convention breakout session for bibliographic instruction. Iannuzzi passes out a worksheet that asks, "What is your topic?" She uses this sheet to help students learn to identify keywords and to teach Boolean searching.

After your trainees have chosen their keywords, have them do an exercise to choose an appropriate database. For example, you can have a one-page exercise in which students match information sought to possible sources.

Then, have each student choose a Web site that could serve as the best subject portal for his or her research area. Make certain that your trainees leave your class equipped with a Web starting point and the keywords they need to do their search.

A More Formal Route

If you want to take a more formal approach to Internet training, you need to define goals, objectives, and measurable or demonstrable outcomes for your training session. Write down the three things that you want to teach. These are your goals. Then, write down three ways that you plan to teach each point. These are your objectives. What should your students know or be able to do after your class? These are your outcomes. At the end of the class, you can ask your students to briefly evaluate your course in writing to see if you have hit your teaching target.

Educational Resources

Academic librarians often offer Web tutorials to reinforce the bibliographic instruction they give to students. Use these resources to get ideas for your own classes.

ICYouSee: T Is For Thinking
www.ithaca.edu/library/Training/hott.html

John R. Henderson, instruction and reference librarian at the Ithaca College Library in New York State, has assembled this useful guide to critical thinking about Web resources. Henderson offers three critical thinking exercises that instructors can use to help students evaluate Web resources.

Finding Information on the Internet: A Tutorial
www.lib.berkeley.edu/TeachingLib/Guides/Internet/
FindInfo.html

Joe Barker, Internet instruction program coordinator at the University of California Teaching Library, assembled this vast and detailed site designed to "provide a current, up-to-date remote and local learning resource for anyone interested in finding information on the World Wide Web." Barker emphasizes "effective,

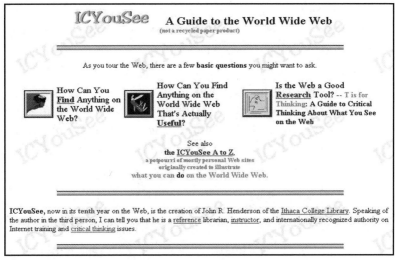

Figure 11.1   Use ICYouSee to help your students understand the Web.

state-of-the-art search strategies applicable to any research interest." This may be more than beginners want to know.

Internet Navigator
www-navigator.utah.edu

This Macromedia Flash site is meant to teach the Internet to the entire state of Utah—well, all the colleges in Utah, anyway. Each college provides a live instructor to help students work through the tutorials.

Internet Tutorials
http://library.albany.edu/internet

Laura Cohen, network services librarian at the University at Albany in New York, maintains this comprehensive, lucid set of Internet tutorials. I particularly appreciate her section called "Understanding the World Wide Web" (http://library.albany.edu/internet/www.html).

Texas Information Literacy Tutorial (TILT)
http://tilt.lib.utsystem.edu

The University of Texas System Digital Library assembled these modules designed to teach information literacy, that is, how to effectively select, search, and evaluate Web resources. Use TILT Lite for slow connections and old computers; Full TILT requires plug-ins for all the bells and whistles.

InFoPeople
www.infopeople.org/index.html

The InFoPeople Project, a partnership of the California State Library and the University of California Berkeley Library, offers this collection of training resources to help libraries in providing public access to the Internet.

LOEX Clearinghouse for Library Instruction
www.emich.edu/public/loex/loex.html

LOEX (Library Orientation Exchange) is a self-supporting, non-profit educational clearinghouse for materials used in library instruction, housed at Eastern Michigan University. Member libraries and librarians have donated all the teaching materials on this site. This is a great resource for training guidance and ideas.

LivingInternet.com
www.livinginternet.com

When introducing newcomers to the Internet, I find it helpful to explain a little bit about its history. This helps my students form a mental model of the Internet and what it can and cannot do. This site covers the important points in the development of the Internet and the World Wide Web and provides interesting quotes from important players.

Glossaries

Define Web terms in your handouts and lectures with the help of these sites.

Webopedia
www.pcwebopedia.com

"The #1 online encyclopedia and search engine dedicated to computer technology," from *PC Magazine*'s experts.

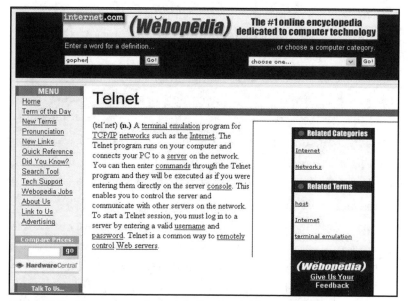

Figure 11.2 Discover ways to explain those weird Internet words at Webopedia.

Matisse's Glossary of Internet Terms
www.matisse.net/files/glossary.html

Matisse Enzer, author of *Unix for Mac OS X* (Peachpit Press, 2002; ISBN 0201795353), assembled this friendly and easy-to-understand Internet lexicon.

Glossary of WWW, Web Searching, and Netscape Jargon
www.lib.berkeley.edu/TeachingLib/Guides/Internet/
Glossary.html

"The Teaching Library" at UC Berkeley offers this glossary as part of their suite of teaching tools.

On the Fly, One-on-One Training

I recently received a very interesting e-mail from Laurie Van Court, reference librarian at the P. S. Miller Library in Castle Rock, Colorado. She wrote, "It's one I suspect reference librarians everywhere are facing, with precious little guidance available in the literature. We are overwhelmed with the pressures of 'OTFOOO': on-the-fly, one-on-one training for our patrons.

"Yes, we can and do offer classes in our lovely labs. But many, many of our patrons will never come to classes. The new Castle Rock library is on the town's main drag, right off the interstate highway. Lots of folks who are just passing through or working in town for the day drop by the library. Some of our hard-won teen patrons view us as the anti-school and would never come in for yet more classes. Moms are time-challenged."

This is a difficult issue. As librarians, we can simplify the interfaces to our catalog and electronic resources and we can print pathfinders to help walk patrons through unfamiliar processes. We can also arrange to have computer-savvy high school or college volunteers come to the library to act as ad-hoc trainers.

Here are some Web sites that explain basic Web concepts simply and are interactively arranged by ascending degrees of difficulty and ease of use. Perhaps we can assemble a collection of these on our library Web sites and direct potential new Internet users there if necessary.

Mouserobics
www.ckls.org/~crippel/computerlab/tutorials/mouse/page1.html

Have a patron who wants to surf the Web but has never used a computer mouse before? Sit him or her down in front of this page to get a little practice.

New User Tutorial
http://tech.tln.lib.mi.us/tutor/welcome.htm

Do you have a patron who has never really used a computer before? Send him or her through this tutorial from the TLN Technology Committee (http://tech.tln.lib.mi.us) written by Andrew Mutch. Also available in Spanish.

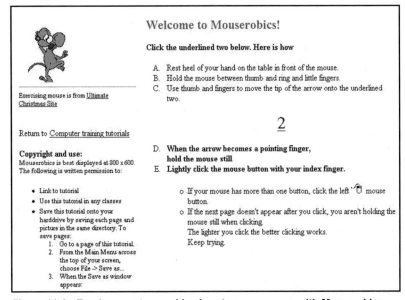

Figure 11.3   Teach computer newbies how to use a mouse with Mouserobics.

Learn the Net
www.learnthenet.com/english/index.html

San Francisco-based Michael Lerner Productions offers these free interactive Web tutorials in English, Spanish, or French. There are lots of great graphics on this site. Have your patrons take the mini-courses "E-mail-at-a-Glance" and "The Web-at-a-Glance."

Computer Training Online
www.ckls.org/~crippel/computerlab/tutorials

Chris Rippel of the Central Kansas Library System in Great Bend has authored this set of explanations, tutorials, and tips about computers and the Web. Rippel covers how to buy and maintain hardware, how to choose software and a bit about how to use it, and articles about how to use the Web and e-mail. This is a great resource with a public library point of view.

Learn the Internet
www.aarp.org/learntech/computers/basic_web

Leave it to the AARP (American Association for Retired Persons) to step up to the plate to teach intrepid seniors how to use the Web. Have patrons start with their basic browsing lessons that cover the tool bar, handling pop-up ads, and printing. Very hip.

ShortGuides.com: Free Computer and Internet Tutorials
http://shortguides.com

Technology trainer and consultant Richard Truxall, based in Ann Arbor, Michigan, has written these concise tutorials and offers them free for all to use. Learn tricky little bits of things like how to use Yahoo! Mail, how to buy a new computer, and how to find your roots online. This could be a very useful site for on-the-fly training handouts.

Internet Tutorials
http://library.albany.edu/internet

Laura Cohen, Network Services Librarian/Webmaster at the University at Albany, one of the State Universities of New York, has written a clear set of computer tutorials that she offers free on this site. New computer-users might enjoy her "How to Copy and Paste from a Web Page to Windows WordPad" or "How to Capture a Graphic on the Web to a Diskette."

DynamicZone FX
www.dzfx.com/workshops/list

This Colorado Web design and marketing company offers free online tutorials for Microsoft Word and other programs. These serve slightly more advanced users. Be aware that the tutorials teach users how to change the home page in Internet Explorer and to customize the navigation buttons. These lessons may be too dangerous for public computer environments!

HowStuffWorks "Internet Channel"
www.howstuffworks.com/category.htm?cat=Intrnt

Atlanta-based HowStuffWorks offers explanation and instruction about every aspect of life on the Internet. Topics range from blogging to cable modems to RSS. Hey, I think that *I* need to spend some time on this site!

Draac.com: A Complete Guide to HTML
www.draac.com

Need to teach a class about how to write fancy Web pages? David Jansen's Draac.com offers tutorials on how to do all of it, from basic HTML to tables, frames, and forms. Jansen's tutorial on CSS is the clearest and cleanest that I have seen.

Those Who Can, Do ... and Teach, Too

All right, maybe I *am* a teacher, in spite of myself. It seems so odd that the main jobs of librarians these days is to: a) Go to meetings, and b) Teach people how to use computers. That may not have been what we expected when we started library school, but it sure gives us job security!

Chapter 12

Making and Maintaining Do-It-Yourself Web Pages

Remember all those little bibliographies, those print pathfinders we librarians love to make to help answer the questions that we get asked over and over, such as, "Where are the tax forms?", "Do you have any biographies?", "Where is your Feng Shui collection?"

Such guides are routine yet useful, and we information professionals feel competent putting them together. Still, these days, we are often compelled to do something for which we may lack the experience or predilection. We are asked to translate our humble pathfinders into computerese, to transform them into Web pages, thus making them universally accessible, independent of time and place. Great idea! But isn't this HTML-ing uncomfortably close to computer programming? Speaking as a reference librarian, I would be more comfortable eating a box of chocolate-covered fire ants than writing a cohesive "go to" statement.

Before we rip up our ALA membership cards in frustration, we need to take a deep breath and remember that basic HTML is easy to figure out. Any effort we put into learning this stuff might well pay off big time, and quickly, too. Think of how we will dazzle our patrons with our computer wizardry—and, more importantly, remind our supervisors of our indispensable flexibility.

First thing to remember: You don't have to be a programmer to write decent HTML. In fact, it's better if you don't try to get too fancy with library pages. The Web is a visual medium, true. Yet, we know that most home computer owners still connect to the Internet over thin phone lines (although more and more folks are connecting through high-speed cable modems and DSL, projected to approach over 50 percent very soon). Our pages, primarily intended to convey information, should be well-designed, but not heavy on the graphics—especially not on moving pictures, which actually consist of a series of stills connected by "applets," little programs that stream down to animate otherwise static pages. Not only can applets take a long time to load, they also consume gobs of processing power on older computers, sometimes freezing them solid.

In general, it is wise to avoid enraging the very people who come to us for answers by burdening them with unnecessarily hefty downloads. On the other hand, we do want our pages interesting and clear, so we want to use a few images and good graphic design. Our real problem becomes not computer programming per se, but rather the practical concerns of taking hyper-text markup language (HTML), a "relatively primitive authoring and layout tool, and beginning to bend and adapt it to a purpose it was never intended to serve: graphic page design," as Patrick J. Lynch, director of the MedMedia Group at the Yale University School of Medicine, puts it in the preface to the first edition of his book *Web Style Guide* (co-author Sarah Horton, Yale University Press, 2nd edition, 2002, ISBN 0300088981, www.webstyleguide.com).

Oh, great. Now, we're not only expected to be writers, publishers, and programmers, but graphic artists, too? You bet we are—and it can be both fun and to our professional advantage to accept the challenge.

So, fire up your browser and prepare to download some tools to help you work your magic. Note that in this chapter, I am not offering a thorough course in the craft of Web page construction. I want to offer an overview, a framework, plus a few tips to give the technological novice a basic understanding of what goes into writing and maintaining a Web page. At the end of this piece, you should be able to make a simple Web page yourself and make changes to your current pages, or at least contribute to discussions about it. Before you begin though, I must reveal my bias toward freeware and shareware for hand-crafting simple pages.

A Different Approach

My fellow columnist at *Searcher* magazine, Dave Rensberger, takes issue with my bargain-conscious approach to Web-page building. In his companion piece to my article, "Make Me a Web Page—Cheap!" (*Searcher*, February 2001, Vol. 9 Issue 2, p. 71), entitled "Pay the $2," Rensberger rightly points out that professional quality software on the market will do your HTML-ing for you. The initial investment of about $400 to $1,200 may seem expensive, but Rensberger points out that "full site management and WYSIWYG ('What You See Is What You Get') authoring tools are a bargain when balanced against the potential management nightmares nonintegrated or highly specialized freeware or shareware packages typically provide."

This is especially true when we try to go interactive with our Web pages, those that can do on-the-fly HTML in response to patron keystrokes. "Most of the deep functionality we see on the Web today really comes from back-end, full-blown programs of a mysterious and complex nature," notes Rensberger. "Making calls to these applications, much less mastering them, can require more resources than you have to invest."

Rensberger recommends three software suites for creating Web pages on Intel-based machines: Dreamweaver from Macromedia (www.macromedia.com/software/dreamweaver), NetObjects Fusion (www.netobjects.com/products/html/nf5. html), and Creative Suite from Adobe (www.adobe.com/products/ creativesuite/main.html). "These are highly integrated packages with great support and consistent interfaces," he says.

Definitely purchase one of these programs if you need to build interactive Web pages or fashion cascading style sheets that provide a consistent look for all the Web pages on a site.

Still, these applications are expensive, complex, and difficult to learn and use. In fact, if our library prefers a polished and professional Web presence, it might be better off outsourcing this task to a professional designer. We librarians who want to make our own basic pages—for pathfinders or teaching aids, for example—like to figure things out for ourselves (or maybe we are just plain cheap). So let's proceed with some tips for hand-crafting our very own Web sites with small assists from inexpensive or free programs available on the Web.

What Is HTML, Exactly?

Visit any Web page. Move your cursor up to the browser toolbar. On either Netscape or Internet Explorer, pull down the "View" menu. Select "Source" or "Page Source." A new window will pop open showing the page surrounded by the otherwise hidden "hyper-text markup language," or HTML, that gives the Web page its look.

Web documents are simply plain-text (also known as ASCII) files that you can create using any text editor such as SimpleText on a Macintosh or Notepad on a Windows machine. In HTML, the important parts of the text document, also known as its "elements," are marked with "tags." Tags allow Web browsers, for example, programs such as Netscape Navigator or Internet Explorer, to recognize component parts of our HTML pages and display them correctly. Examples of elements include heads, tables, paragraphs, and lists.

Tags are words enclosed between "less-than" and "greater-than" symbols, that is, "<" and ">." Tags almost always come in pairs. The opening tag defines the beginning of an element; the second, or ending tag, marks the place where the element stops. For example, all Web documents begin with the tag <html> and end with the tag </html>. (Notice the right slash after the less-than sign on the closing tag.) This set of tags tells the browser that the document is a Web page and allows it to interpret the file accordingly.

All Web pages must have several essential tags. When typed out on a text editor, they look like this:

```
<html>
<head>
<title>Web Site Title</title>
</head>
<body>
Contents of Web Site
</body>
</html>
```

At the beginning and end of the file, notice those <html> tags. Within this set of tags are two other tag sets: the head and the body. The head section contains information that surfers don't see, but that browsers can read. The "metadata" that search engines use to classify pages is often hidden in the document head. The head also must contain the Web page title, marked by the <title></title> tags.

Below the head lies the body section of the document. All the text and pictures that site visitors actually *see* is sandwiched between these two <body></body> tags.

HTML is based on an earlier and more complicated publishing layout standard called "Standard Generalized Markup Language," or SGML. It has also spawned a new, evolving standard called "eXtensible Markup Language," or XML. HTML and XML standards are "interoperable," that is, they work on the same principles and use many of the same markup tags. The difference is that tags in HTML serve as crude tools for Web page layout and hypertext linking. For example, text on a document written in HTML will display in the center of a line if it appears enclosed in the   tags. In contrast, the tags in XML act as a way to define the content and structure of a document. For instance, the author of a document can be marked as an "author" element, for example, <author>Jane Doe</author>.

This content tagging allows software to easily "parse" documents. This means that all kinds of programs can recognize the different sections and elements within a document. The tagged data can be easily pulled out, indexed, and displayed according to the preferences of an end-user.

XML does not replace HTML. HTML sets up how a Web page *looks*. In contrast, XML tags are invisible on a Web page and don't actually *do* anything—they simply describe the pieces of information on the page. The purpose of including XML definitions on a Web page is to allow the data on it to be more understandable and usable across different hardware systems, programming languages, and software.

HTML and XML are designed to complement each other. In fact, a Web page that is laid out using HTML and that also follows the rules of XML is said to be written in "XHTML." XHTML is very strict about its tags and structure. Because of that discipline, it can be used by XML-enabled devices and Internet mobile phones, and is backward-compatible with any old browser. It is no wonder that Web pages written in XHTML are considered "well-formed"!

We can start writing our Web pages in XHTML today. To learn more about this standard, and how it differs from regular HTML, visit the World Wide Web Consortium page on XHTML Standards (www.w3.org/TR/xhtml1/#diffs).

To learn more about XML and how it applies in the real world, visit the fine XML Tutorial (www.w3schools.com/xml/default.asp) from Refsnes Data, a Norwegian software development and consulting company.

If you see layouts or colors that please you on another Web page, take a look at the source code to see how they did it. You might even borrow bits of useful HTML to plug in to your own HTML code. Be careful about taking images, though. Those may well be under copyright.

HTML Reference

I am pleased to report that no knowledge of SGML or computer programming is required to make a basic Web page. Still, you might want more information as to what this whole HTML thing is all about and how to use it. These sites can point you in the right direction.

NCSA Beginner's Guide to HTML
http://archive.ncsa.uiuc.edu/General/Internet/WWW/
HTMLPrimer.html

The National Center for Supercomputing Applications at the University of Illinois at Urbana-Champaign, birthplace of the first graphical Web browser, has offered this beginner's guide since the Web was first woven. Web fanciness has exploded since then, but the basic idea remains the same. If you need to write a library page primarily intended to get information to your patrons, this guide will teach you everything you need to know.

WDVL: The Beginners Page
www.wdvl.com/WebRef/Help/Begin.html

Internet.com's Web Developer's Virtual Library is a great place to visit when faced with the need to construct a Web page for the first time. It begins with explanations of the Internet, the World Wide Web, and HTML, and leads to a catalog of Web-based tutorials.

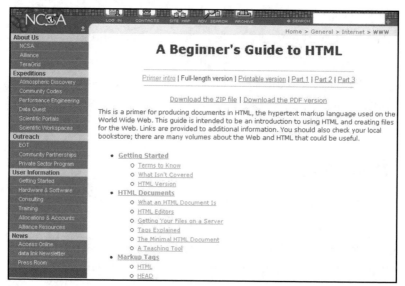

Figure 12.1 Learn to write HTML with the HTML Primer from NCSA.

HTML Tutor
www.december.com/html/tutor

Milwaukee-based Web instructor John December has put his lessons on the Web. These range from the most basic to more advanced tutorials.

HTML Cheatsheet from Webmonkey
http://webmonkey.wired.com/webmonkey/reference/
html_cheatsheet

Refer to this cheatsheet whenever you forget how to write that HTML tag that you planned to use.

Web Design for Librarians
www.scc.rutgers.edu/scchome_old/policies/web.htm

Rutgers University data librarian Ron Jantz has culled the juicy bits from many Web design guidelines. His guide pulls together the best of current Web design thinking, revealing wisdom such as "Reading from computer screens is 25 percent slower than from paper" and "Web content should be 50 percent the size of its paper equivalent." Jantz also points to many full-text resources on the Web.

Web Style Guide
www.webstyleguide.com

If you really want to know what it means to design a Web page to deliver content effectively, study this guide, written by Patrick J. Lynch, Director of the MedMedia Group at the Yale University School of Medicine, and Sarah Horton, Instructional Technology Specialist at Dartmouth College.

HTML Editors

Now you know how HTML works, but you don't want to type out all those tags yourself, even though you *could* with any plain text editor. Caution: Never use formal word processing programs like Microsoft Word to build or edit a Web page. These applications always add gobs of their own hidden formatting code to your text. This formatting just doesn't translate to the Web and is very hard to remove once it is there. Instead, go out on the Internet and download some specialized HTML-writing software to make the whole Web-page crafting process a lot easier.

Notetab Light
www.notetab.com/ntl.php

This sturdy, free program for PCs is essentially a text editing application with HTML writing aids attached. After the program opens, click on the HTML tab along the bottom of the opening screen. Then, click on "New Web Page" near the top of the column on the left. This will generate a simple template on the editing screen that automatically forms the "bones" of a basic Web page. If you know nothing about HTML, read the NCSA Beginner's Guide to HTML (www.ncsa.uiuc.edu/General/Internet/WWW/HTML Primer.html) before beginning.

HTML Creator
http://tmdc.org/htmlcreator

Apple Macintosh users, rejoice! Aram Kudurshian has solved your Web page building problems by creating a bargain HTML editor just for you. This highly rated program has a "Scratch Pad" where you can save bits of code to drag into any open HTML document. Send Mr. Kudurshian a measly $15 to register your copy. Such a Mac deal!

Choosing Color

A good Web page makes strategic use of color. Some fortunate folks are born with a natural color sense, but, sadly, I am not among them. I need assistance in selecting attractive, harmonious, yet sufficiently contrasting color combinations for my background, text, links, and so on.

Note that, in HTML, colors are usually represented by a six-digit code called a hexadecimal representation, or hex code. It looks like this: #RRGGBB, where RR, GG, and BB are the hexadecimal values for the red, green, and blue values of the color. When there is no color at all, that is, when you want black, the color code is #000000, because black has no red, green or blue. When all three colors are turned up full force, for example, #FFFFFF, the color you get is white.

Older computers are limited in the number of colors they can portray. When they need to render a color outside the usual, they do it by interspersing dots of different colors, hoping that they will blend. This is called "dithering" and it isn't pretty. Also, PC-based computers display colors differently than Macs do. The solution, when designing a Web page, has been to choose among the 216 colors on the "Web-safe palette," that is, the colors that will appear smooth and clean no matter what computer monitor displays them.

Color Combinations: Color, Creativity, Code
www.worqx.com/color/combinations.htm

All right, now that we realize that we have 216 colors to choose from, how can we decide which to use on our page? Here is a simple yet beautiful tutorial about color theory, the idea that colors have relationships to each other, which you can see illustrated when the hues are arranged around a wheel. Worqx also discusses the role of shade, which is the amount of black added to a pure color, and tint, which measures how much a color is diluted with white.

VisiBone Webmaster's Color Lab
www.visibone.com/colorlab

VisiBone has arranged the 216-color Web-safe palette in a useful color wheel. Choose contrasting, triad, or tertiary tones, then see how they play together on a panel to the side. See the 216 colors laid out in a flat chart at http://html-color-codes.com. VisiBone gives the hex code for every color so users can just type the exact colors that they chose into their HTML tags.

Color Scheme Generator 2
http://wellstyled.com/tools/colorscheme2/index-en.html

Czech Web designer Petr Staníče gives us this online color wheel that can be set to use only a Web-safe palette. Simply click on a color on the wheel and then choose the harmonious color accent scheme that you prefer: mono, contrast, triad, tetrad, or analogic. See these palettes in their dark, light, and medium pastel manifestations. Use the pull-down menu to see how these color combos would appear to users with various types of colorblindness. When you have found the scheme that you wish to use, simply harvest the hex codes on the right side of the screen. This is a remarkable tool.

Spin the Colour Wheel
www.webwhirlers.com/colors/wheel.asp

Still can't decide which colors to use? Donald Johansson offers this online application that serves up random sets of three colors

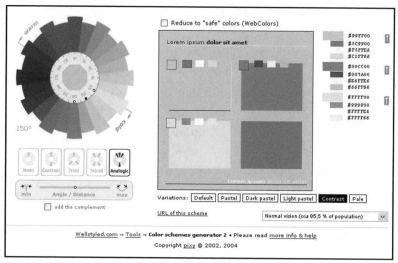

Figure 12.2   Use this online color wheel from WellStyled.com to find harmonious hues in a Web-safe palette.

that look very well together. Simply designate which of the three should be the background, the secondary color, and the text and then see how the colors would look on a real Web page.

Image Editors

Now that we have chosen a color scheme for our Web site that is both delightful and compelling, all that remains is to add a few images. Just as a word processor allows us to change text, an image editor gives us the power to fix pictures. Here are a few good ones offered free or at reasonable prices.

Paint Shop Pro
www.corel.com

This is my favorite image editor for the PC. Developed by Jasc Software but now owned by CorelCorp., this shareware product costs $130, but is similar in feel and utility to products costing over six times as much. Download a 30-day trial for free, and then get your boss to buy it for you.

IrfanView
www.irfanview.com

Bosnian native Irfan Skiljan gives PC users this multimedia editing software free for noncommercial use. It captures, crops, and
adds special effects. It even works on movie files. *ZDNet* gives this
program its highest rating and says, "Make no mistake about it—
IrfanView is a true freeware gem." Commercial users, please send
Mr. Skiljan $10 to register your program.

FuturePaint
www.stazsoftware.com/shareware/index.php?category=graphics

Here is that most rare of freeware gems: a graphics program for
the Mac. As its download page on the STAZ Software site boasts:
"Move over, Photoshop! There's a new kid in town and he's got pixel
power to spare!" Works only in Classic.

GraphicConverter
www.lemkesoft.de/en/graphcon.htm

Germany's Thorsten Lemke watches over Mac users with this
image manipulation program. GraphicConverter costs $30, but is
worth much more, as it offers you plenty of control over your
images, including an impressive array of special effects.

ImageJ
http://rsb.info.nih.gov/ij/index.html

Wayne Rasband and the National Institutes of Health have
developed this Java-based text editor. It will run on any platform:
all Mac versions, and PC- or Unix-based computers. Because its
development is taxpayer supported, you can get it for free.

GIFWorks
www.gifworks.com

You have used your image editors to craft some great pictures
for your library pages. Now, it's time to slim them down so they will
slide quickly over the phone lines to your patron's computers.
Make your digital images as small as possible with image opti-
mization software like GIFWorks. Point this Web-based image editor at your .gif file, and it will gradually decrease the number of

colors in the picture. Choose the image with the smallest file size that still retains an acceptable image quality. This program is Web-based and thus platform independent. The best news of all: It's completely free!

Free Fonts

Along with images, you can use some funky type fonts to jazz up your site. A font usually comes down from the Web as a compressed file. PC users can unpack this file with the free "Zip Reader" program from PKWARE (www.pkware.com/satellite-o/free_zip_program. php). Then, they can move the unzipped file to their system font folder located in the Control Panel. Mac users can use the free "Stuffit Expander" (www.stuffit.com/mac/expander/index. html) to open up a new font file.

Larabie Fonts
www.myfonts.com/browse/foundry/larabie
Canadian Ray Larabie has created almost 400 fonts and offers them for free in both PC and Mac versions. These fonts are easy to read, yet stylish. Larabie has joined forces with MyFonts.com. Yet he still offers his fonts gratis in return for registration. Larabie also offers fonts for sale on the site.

Fontcraft's Scriptorium Fonts and Graphic Arts
www.ragnarokpress.com/scriptorium/index.html
Ragnarok Press offers commercial and some shareware fonts (www.fontcraft.com/scriptorium/month.html) for those who prefer an old-fashioned look on their Web pages. Come here to find medieval, gothic, script, and arts-and-crafts type fonts and page borders for both Macs and PCs. Read their article "Effective Use of Fonts in Web Design" (www.fontcraft.com/scriptorium/wfarticle. html) for some terrific tips.

Figure 12.3   Visit Font Diner for some fine '50s fonts.

Font Diner
www.fontdiner.com/main.html

How about some fine Fifties-style fonts? Get 'em here, while they are hot.

Famous Fonts at SharkShock
www.sharkshock.com/fonts/fontsfoo.html

Dennis Ludlow has collected these free famous-looking fonts for the PC. Here are famous food fonts, for example, one that resembles the logo of Dr. Pepper, and fonts used for games, cars, companies, sports teams, and shows, for example a font that looks like the writing for *Gilligan's Island*. Mac users can convert these Windows fonts by downloading a trial version of a program called "TransType" (www.fontlab.com/Font-tools/TransType).

Blue Vinyl Fonts
www.bvfonts.com

Hep cats come to Blue Vinyl Fonts for free and very reasonably priced retro-looking fonts.

File Transfer Programs

Once you have your HTML and image files ready on your hard drive, how do you get them up to your server so they can go out on the Web? Why, with a "file transfer protocol," or ftp program, of course. Here are some clients for both PCs and Macs.

Cute FTP
www.cuteftp.com

According to the editors at CNET.com, the best FTP client for Windows is CuteFTP by GlobalSCAPE, Inc. "CuteFTP is the best transfer utility on the market," they declare. "It's easy enough for newbies yet tough enough for seasoned file movers." Try it for 30 days free, but then cough up the $39.95 for this dependable, indispensable FTP program.

SmartFTP
www.smartftp.com

You can use this FTP program for Windows for free, but a license that includes a year of support costs about $37. SmartFTP can make the "secure" connection required by some ISPs and comes in more than 20 languages.

FTP Voyager
www.ftpvoyager.com

International PC-based Web page builders, try this multilingual FTP client. For less than $50, you can register your copy of this award-winning program in English, Spanish, German, French, Finnish, Italian, Korean, Russian, Chinese, or Japanese. Try it for 30 days free first.

Fetch
http://fetchsoftworks.com

Fetch is an easy-to-use, full-featured FTP client for the Apple Macintosh. A single user license to Fetch is $25, but you can try it for free for 15 days.

Testers and Fixers

So, how can you tell if your newly learned HTML skills are up to snuff? Are there any loose ends on those pages you just painstakingly assembled? It's nice to know that proofreading tools exist out there to help us comb through our coding and get out the kinks.

Viewable with Any Browser
www.anybrowser.org/campaign/index.html

Cari D. Burstein sponsors this campaign to simplify Web pages and make them accessible with any browser, not just the latest edition of Internet Explorer. This is a great resource for library Webmasters interested in providing straightforward information for use on every operating system.

HTML Tidy Online
http://infohound.net/tidy

After you have cobbled together your Web page, paste its HTML here. Or, check a page already online. HTML Tidy will tell you where your mistakes are and advise you how to make your page more accessible. You don't even have to fix the code yourself. Simply download the cleaned-up version from the site, all courtesy of Australian programmer Jonathan Hedley.

Xenu's Link Sleuth
http://home.snafu.de/tilman/xenulink.html

Say your Web site has been up for a while now and you begin to notice that it has started looking a little shabby. Some of the links don't work anymore, for instance. Do you want to test each link individually to see if it has changed? No! Instead, download the freeware for PCs called Xenu, offered by German programmer Tilman Hausherr. Xenu can check just one page or the whole site. This spidering software verifies "normal" links, images, frames, plug-ins, backgrounds, local image maps, style sheets, scripts, and java applets.

Give Me More!

Ah, now that your appetite is whetted for fame and glory as a Web-page designer, where do you go for more tricks and tips? There are plenty of helpful sites on the Web, and here are a few of my favorites.

Web Developers' Virtual Library
http://wdvl.internet.com

Internet.com brings us this comprehensive group of Web-building resources for all levels of competence.

Webmonkey
http://webmonkey.wired.com/webmonkey

Lycos sponsors Webmonkey: The Web Developer's Resource. Visit the top right part of this opening page and click on the link for "Beginners." View a "How-to Library" to help you move beyond the basics into making wild stuff like tables and frames. Yikes!

BigNoseBird
www.bignosebird.com

Bruce Gronich has a mission: providing Web-authoring information and assistance to novice and intermediate Webmasters. He succeeds admirably on this friendly, helpful site. The "big nose bird" is how his 3-year-old insisted on describing an ibis.

Reallybig.com Web Builder Network
http://reallybig.com/default.php3

This site offers more than 5,000 resources for Web-site builders including free clip art, CGI, counters, fonts, HTML, Java, animation, backgrounds, icons, WYSIWYG (What You See Is What You Get) editors, buttons, photographs, site promotion, and much more. Reallybig calls itself "The Complete Resource for anyone who wants to create pages on the Internet, from beginner to experienced Web site developer." This is a site of riches free for the taking.

Si, Se Puede!

Yes, you may have to put out a little cash and invest some time in climbing the old learning curve, but now you have enough information to sit down and make your own Web page. No more whining! I want to see that page (perhaps providing a bibliography or pathfinder information?) up within the month. Can we librarians fashion our own Web pages, thus saving trees, that is, paper, for printing handouts and making our contribution to the Information Age? Yes, we can!

Chapter 13

Making the Web Accessible to the Disabled

"The power of the Web is in its universality. Access
by everyone regardless of disability is an essential aspect."
–Tim Berners-Lee,
W3C Director and inventor of the World Wide Web

I remember when I was pregnant, waddling around UCLA, trying to get my master's degree. My assigned parking garage lay at least a mile down the hill from the library school building. Every day, after driving across Los Angeles for more than an hour, I'd unwedge myself from my car, strap my books to a luggage cart, and start the long struggle up the hill to hear yet another fascinating lecture on database construction or some other equally compelling topic. I was not a happy pregnant person. I was hormonally irritable and had sharp, stabbing sciatica running down the back of my right leg. That being said, if I encountered any barrier on my journey up to class, you can bet I gave it a profane, if *sotto voce*, dressing down.

I learned to appreciate—no, *insist* upon—curb cuts, ramps, and other aids to my mobility. The switchback trail laid out as the handicapped access path across UCLA, invisible to me just months before, stood out like neon. This was my physical lifeline, the golden route that allowed my achy, cranky body to get to class and finish my degree.

Just as wheelchair ramps make buildings accessible to those with mobility problems, the Web should make information accessible to people with all kinds of disabilities. To a certain degree, it already does. Still, to those who use assistive devices to surf, many pages are difficult, if not impossible, to navigate. Imagine that you are blind and using a screen reader to hear a Web page. Suddenly, you come across a piece of Java script. It has been said that hearing Java read aloud is like listening to Martian poetry. It is certainly not communicating the message that the author intended. We often think of the Web as a visual medium. Yet, as a practical matter, we use it as a medium for information of all kinds.

Types of Disabilities

The U.S. Census Bureau reports that, at the last census, almost 50 million people identified themselves as disabled (www.census. gov/Press-Release/www/2002/cb02ff11.html). This is a full 19 percent of the population, or one person in five. Most of these conditions make it difficult to use the Web as we know it.

Those with low vision need screen magnifiers or large print to understand a page. The completely "print disabled" need screen readers to hear Web information, along with mouse keyboard support. Users can't move a mouse to point and click if they can't see the monitor.

Those with physical impairments may have trouble manipulating a mouse (especially elderly users with shaky hands) or pushing more than one key at a time, for example, *Alt-F*. Or maybe they have trouble pushing a single key, in which case a keyguard would come in handy. Some folks can't use their hands at all and need membrane keyboards they can poke with mouth sticks.

The hearing-impaired miss out on audio or video clips that lack captions.

Cognitive disorders include dyslexia, an inability to make sense of written words.

Finally, there are plenty of people—far exceeding one-fifth of the population—who never learned to type (think retired executives), can't read English, or maybe just can't get this whole Internet thing straight in their heads. I teach plenty of patrons who type in the Yahoo! address and then can't get past the banner ads. "Why did I get this? This is not what I asked for!" The whole idea of "scroll down" is a remarkably difficult concept to grasp for folks who have not used a computer before.

When you think about it, there are so many reasons why the Web can seem obscure that it's amazing that anyone can use it at all.

Inclusive Web Design

How can we help our disabled patrons get all the information they need from the Web? The regional librarian for the blind and physically handicapped at the Cleveland Public Library, Barbara T. Mates, writes, "One of the very first goals is making your Web site accessible. Be sure that people using adaptive equipment to access the Internet are not faced with obstacles. This is not a costly measure and could be acted on immediately" (www.ala.org/ala/products/books/editions/matesadaptivetechnologyinternetch12.htm).

How can we do this? First, simply remember to include a text alternative to every graphical element on your page. In HTML, it looks something like this: *<img src="../images/smplbanner.gif" alt="San Marino Public Library top banner">*. Those using screen-readers to surf the Web can then hear what they can't see. In fact, the latest HTML standards require this "alt" tag for all images.

Screen readers display Web pages sequentially. That means that tables written in HTML must employ clear row and column headings if we want them to make any sense to the visually impaired. Frames do not translate well on screen readers either. Every frame must have a meaningful title to help users move easily to the content that they want to read. Design your forms, too, with the screen-reading public in mind. For more specific information on the proper tags to use for accessible frames, tables, and forms, take a look at "Web Accessibility Makeover" (www-306.ibm.com/able/dwnlds/WebAccessibilityMakeover.ppt), a PowerPoint presentation written by Shannon Rapuano of IBM Accessibility Center and Don Barrett, Department of Education.

We may use Java elements on our Web pages, but we should use Sun's Java "Accessibility API" (http://java.sun.com/products/jfc/accessibility/index.jsp) to design them. The Accessibility API offers a way for Java applications to work with assistive technology such as voice recognition or screen magnifiers. ("API" stands for Application Program Interface. It refers to standardized blocks of code that programmers can plug into their work to make their applications compliant with specific operating systems and conditions.)

CSS: Cascading Style Sheets

We can also make our Web pages more accessible by writing them using Cascading Style Sheets, or CSS.

The basic idea about HTML is that it separates content from presentation. That is, we write what we write and let our readers' computers worry about the layout. There are a couple of problems with that. First, as page designers, we would really like to have some control over the *look* of our pages as well as the words on the page. Second, in HTML, to change the look of our site means having to edit every page, because the formatting code, that is, the HTML tags that determine the layout of a Web page, are embedded in each file.

What if we could accompany the HTML files that we store on our Web server with a small text file that contains most of the formatting tags for the whole site? The <head></head> part of our content-bearing Web pages would contain a tag that links to this little file. When we want to make a change to our site, to alter a font color, say, we could make the change in the little file. This update in *style* would then *cascade* across our entire Web site. Get it?

The tag in the <head></head> part of a Web page that links to the little text file looks something like this: <link href="../styles.css" rel="stylesheet" type="text/css" />. In this case, the little text file with all the formatting in it is named "styles.css". It could be called anything, as long as the file extension is .css.

Most new browsers support this linking to a style sheet. On old browsers—or even on cell phone Web browsers—Web pages written with CSS display their full-text content in sequential order, simply eliminating the fancy colors and layout. Screen readers can read these simplified pages easily without having to say quite so many tags out loud.

CSS offers another accessibility advantage. One Web page can offer several links to different style sheets. The default style sheet may suit most people, but those with low vision might choose a look that offers larger print, perhaps in high contrast. The change in display can be made by users instantly, with the click of a link. How cool is that? For an example of a Web page that uses three style sheets to offer small, medium, or large text size, visit Usability First (www.usabilityfirst.com).

CSS strongly corresponds with, and in many ways conforms to, many of the principles and rules of XML (www.w3.org/XML). Still, if the idea of both CSS and XML are relatively simple, the actual syntax can be hard to figure out. Here are some CSS tutorials that try to explain the whole thing.

Draac.Com's CSS Course
www.draac.com/css/css1.html

Draac.com offers tutorials on many aspects of building Web pages. Their tutorial on CSS is the clearest and cleanest that I have seen.

Figure 13.1   Read the tutorial at Draac.com to learn how to create CSS.

Webmonkey Reference: Style Sheet Guide
http://webmonkey.wired.com/webmonkey/reference/
stylesheet_guide

Wired magazine's Webmonkey explains CSS to all of us.

Holy CSS, Zeldman!
www.dezwozhere.com/links.html

Andrew Fernandez has collected a whole bunch of links to CSS-related tutorials.

Style Master CSS Editor
www.westciv.com/style_master

This program works on both PCs and Macs to help users make style sheets for their Web pages. Try it for free; buy it for $60.

Mulder's Stylesheets Tutorials
http://webmonkey.wired.com/webmonkey/authoring/stylesheets/
tutorials/tutorial1.html

Lycos' Steve Mulder, author of *Web Designer's Guide to Style Sheets* (Macmillan Computer, 1997, ISBN 1568303068), created this five-day style-sheet tutorial.

Accessibility Portals

Plenty of sites offer advice on accessible technology in general and inclusive Web design in particular. Here are some of the best.

WebABLE

www.webable.com

WebABLE is a directory of adaptive technologies. Browse the library of books and articles that focus on accessibility or drill down in the directory of categorized links of tools and utilities. I particularly like the Web accessibility design tips that appear on the right side of the page.

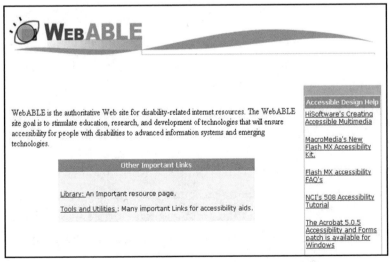

Figure 13.2   Browse WebABLE, a directory of adaptive technologies.

Alliance for Technology Access
www.ataccess.org

The Alliance for Technology Access, or ATA, exists for the purpose of "connecting children and adults with disabilities to technology tools." The handsome and easy-to-negotiate page offers up-to-date links to a variety of assistive technology resources, including sources for grant money. The ATA site also includes some very good advice on accessible Web page design (www.ataccess.org/rresources/webaccess.html).

DO-IT Program
www.washington.edu/doit

The University of Washington sponsors the Disabilities, Opportunities, Internetworking & Technology (DO-IT) program. Visit their list of links to resources for accessible Web design (www.washington.edu/doit/Resources/accessweb.html).

Center on Disabilities
www.csun.edu/cod

The California State University at Northridge offers this program that helps disabled students and also sponsors the yearly "Technology and Persons with Disabilities" conference. The conference exhibits offer a fantastic place to sample all the latest in assistive technologies. The Center on Disabilities site offers a good example of assistive-technology-friendly Web design.

AWARE Center
aware.hwg.org

AWARE stands for "Accessible Web Authoring Resources and Education." The HTML Writers Guild sponsors this site whose mission is to serve as a central resource for Web authors learning about Web accessibility. Click through their comprehensive list of important resources for Web authors creating accessible pages.

Web Accessibility Initiative (WAI)
www.w3.org/WAI

The World Wide Web Consortium (W3C) sponsors this program to promote its interest in Web accessibility. Under the direction of Judy Brewer, director of the Web Accessibility Initiative International Program Office, the WAI team develops resources that increase the accessibility of the Web, including guidelines for Web page content, browsers, and authoring tools.

Adaptive Technology for the Internet
www.ala.org/ala/products/books/editions/
adaptivetechnology.htm

In her book, *Adaptive Technology for the Internet,* now only available online, the regional librarian for the blind and physically handicapped at the Cleveland Public Library, Barbara T. Mates, asks the question, "Could Helen Keller use your library?" Get Mates's take on ways to make the Internet more accessible for our visually and physically challenged patrons.

Designing More Useable Web Sites
http://trace.wisc.edu/world/web

The Trace Center of the College of Engineering at the University of Wisconsin at Madison is dedicated to making technology more user-friendly. Their page provides links to help us build accessibility into our Web pages.

The Adaptive Technology Resource Centre (ATRC)
www.utoronto.ca/atrc

The University of Toronto sponsors this program that works directly with information technology manufacturers and developers to influence the early design stages of computer-based technology. The ATRC looks for technology solutions that are commercially feasible, operationally effective, and universally accessible. Check out the "Technical Glossary" (www.utoronto.ca/atrc/reference/tech/techgloss.html), an annotated directory of currently available assistive technologies and their vendors.

IBM Accessibility Center
www-306.com/able

IBM offers this portal to help businesses become more accessible in general and reach people with disabilities. This portal has advice on employment law and offers adaptive computer technologies to aid with most disabilities. Here, IBM sells voice recognition software and a Web browser able to read pages aloud. Download the 30-day trial version of this software, called Home Page Reader (www-306.ibm.com/able/solution_offerings/hpr. html). Test your pages on it to see how they would sound to a blind person.

Tools and Utilities

Some software, please, to help us improve our Web pages.

Watchfire WebXACT
http://webxact.watchfire.com

This online application, formerly known as Bobby, allows users to check Web pages to ensure they are free from significant barriers to access by individuals with disabilities. Since WebXACT's guidelines conform to anyone's standard of good Web page design, we should probably test all our HTML pages with it. For no charge, WebXACT will analyze one Web page at a time for quality, accessibility, and privacy issues, and then generate an in-depth report. Elsewhere on its site, Watchfire sells similar accessibility-checking software for large organizations.

A-Prompt Project
http://aprompt.snow.utoronto.ca

The Adaptive Technology Resource Centre (ATRC) at the University of Toronto and the Trace Center at the University of Wisconsin have developed this accessibility validator. Download this PC-compatible freeware and use it to check your HTML as you write.

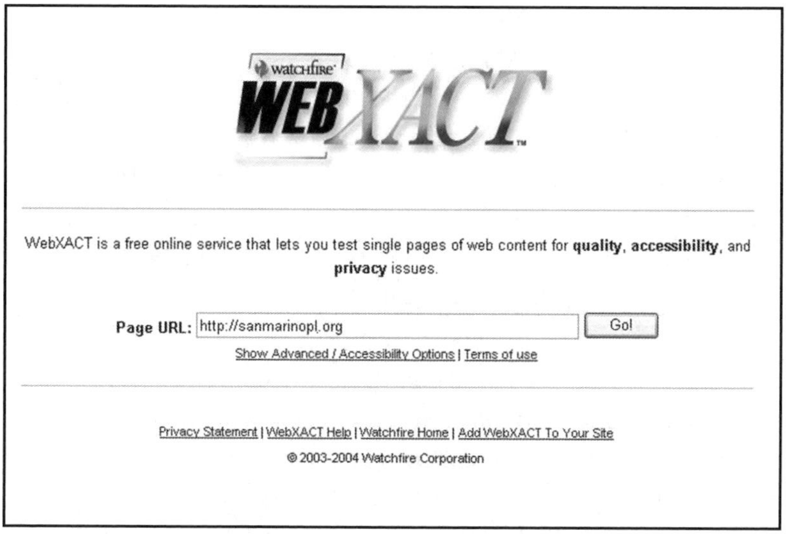

Figure 13.3   An accessible page is a well-designed page. Test yours with WebXACT.

Accessible Web Publishing Wizard for Microsoft Office
http://cita.rehab.uiuc.edu/software/office/index.html

The Division of Rehabilitation Education Services at the University of Illinois at Urbana/Champaign wrote this program that easily converts Microsoft Word, Excel spreadsheets, and even PowerPoint presentations into accessible and valid HTML 4.01 with CSS, that is, a Web page accessible to all. Microsoft's own Web-page conversion software has a problem: It adds tremendous amounts of unnecessary code to what should be a simple HTML document. This application, originating from a third party, avoids that pitfall. Try it for free and then buy it for $40 or less per license.

VisCheck Color Blindness Simulator
www.vischeck.com/daltonize

Research has shown that one out of every 10 males has difficulty seeing color and that one in five people has some form of vision impairment. How can we guarantee that most of our patrons can see the color we use on our Web pages? Robert Dougherty and Alex

Wade, two vision scientists at Stanford University, have developed VisCheck, an online or downloadable program for PCs. VisCheck is a vision simulator that lets you see how your images look to those with various kinds of dichromatic limitations.

Colorblind users: Try Daltonize (www.vischeck.com/daltonize), a free online or downloadable application for PCs that processes images to correct for different types of colorblindness.

Media Access Generator (MAGpie)
http://ncam.wgbh.org/webaccess/magpie

Make your Web-mounted audios and videos accessible to those without access to sound by using captions generated by this program. Using MAGpie, Web developers can add captions to three multimedia formats: Apple's QuickTime (www.apple.com/quicktime), the World Wide Web Consortium's Synchronized Multimedia Integration Language (SMIL, www.w3.org/AudioVideo), and Microsoft's Synchronized Accessible Media Interchange (SAMI, www.msdn.microsoft.com/library/en-us/dnacc/html/atg_sami article.asp?frame=true). MAGpie comes from the Trace Research and Development Center at the University of Wisconsin, as part of its Information Technology Access Rehabilitation Engineering Research Center, funded by the U.S. Department of Education's National Institute on Disability and Rehabilitation Research.

More Assistive Technologies

In addition to fixing our Web pages, we can offer workstations in the library that are handicapped accessible. These software products can help.

Microsoft Accessibility Home
www.microsoft.com/enable

A few yeas ago, when the state of Massachusetts and the federal government told Microsoft that they could not purchase the new operating system for their hundreds of thousands of employees due to laws requiring equal access in the public workplace, Microsoft added features to Windows 95 that provide a multitude of input and output alternatives for a broad range of users, not just the disabled.

The point? When users band together in a big enough economic group, commercial forces respond. This has definitely been the case with the Microsoft Corporation, which has added a whole hub of articles and applications designed to make its products more usable for disabled customers. I enjoyed reading the section for Baby Boomers: "Aging and Accessible Technology: How Accessible Technology Can Help Aging Workers Retain High Productivity" (www.microsoft.com/enable/aging/default.aspx). I had to make the type size larger to read it, of course.

Simply Internet 2000
www.econointl.com/sw

Sergio Ammirata brings us this freeware program for PCs that makes newer versions of Internet Explorer talk via a software-based speech synthesizer. Bring your headphones—the Web has something to tell you.

Opera
www.opera.com

Opera is a Web browser trying to make inroads into Internet Explorer territory. While not strictly a browser for special needs access, the Opera does support CSS style sheets, and offers the ability to toggle frames on and off, control zooming, and specify font color. It works in both PC and UNIX environments. Use the ad-supported version for free, or pay $10 to buy a license.

YSpeak
www.stazsoftware.com/yspeak

STAZ Software brings you this free text-to-speech synthesizer designed especially for the Apple i-Book laptop computer, although it will run on almost any Mac. YSpeak will speak typed input in any one of 25 different voices, both male and female. For those who have difficulty typing, YSpeak offers an on-screen keyboard and word predicting software. Files saved to the disk can be converted and read by all standard word processing programs. Although the author of YSpeak, Phil Yates, died of Amyotrophic Lateral Sclerosis (ALS, "Lou Gehrig's disease") in 2001, STAZ Software continues to host and support his program.

Apple: Accessibility
www.apple.com/accessibility

Here, Apple offers help for disabled Mac users. Click on one of the five major categories of functional limitations listed on the navigation bar to see which accessibility features in Mac OS X address it. These pages also include information about third party Macintosh compatible applications that can also help.

Where to Buy

When you need to buy adaptive technology hardware to make those workstations truly accessible, try these sites.

The Boulevard: An Assistive Technology Expo
www.blvd.com

Visit this giant shopping directory to find the accessories you will need to make your library truly accessible.

EnableMart
www.enablemart.com

Libraries that need to make their technology accessible to all should visit this shopping portal. EnableMart accepts purchase orders, making it easy for government and educational institutions to buy from them.

Infogrip
www.infogrip.com

Infogrip not only sells accessible workstations, it offers consultation and even presentations about ADA compliance for libraries.

Pulse Data International
www.pulsedata.com

Pulse Data, formerly known as HumanWare, is a major distributor of print-access technologies for the blind and people with low vision or other reading or learning disabilities. Look here for Braille readers and writers and magnifying software for those with low vision.

Words+
www.words-plus.com

Words+ sells "augmentive communication devices" to such luminaries as Dr. Stephen Hawking. Find everything here from sensitive keyboards to devices that let you control your computer with a sharp breath or the blinking of an eye. Get devices that will talk for you, too.

Making Electronic Resources Accessible in the Library

Barbara T. Mates is a librarian who knows how to make her resources accessible. In the online version of her book, *Adaptive Technology for the Internet* (ALA Editions, 1999, ISBN 0838907520, www.ala.org/ala/products/books/editions/adaptivetechnology. htm), Mates offers matter-of-fact advice on all kinds of technologies to help disabled patrons use electronic resources in the library.

Tops on her to-do list, after getting the Web site fixed, is to find out what accessibility products you already have and then implement training and procedures on using them. "For instance," she writes, "users who are deaf would be aided by Microsoft's SoundSentry alerting device, but would they know it's available and could be activated?"

Mates advises libraries to purchase computer monitors that measure at least 19 inches diagonally. Also, she suggests that we equip keyboards with large print keytop labels and buy some screen-enlarging software and printers that can handle large print.

We should prepare adaptive workstations and put them in a prominent place in the library so that people using wheelchairs or walkers can find them. Equip these stations with screen-reader technologies and alternate input devices such as a speech-recognition system, a trackball, or a membrane keyboard.

These modifications will go a long way to help people with all kinds of physical or learning disabilities to access the Internet and other electronic resources in the library, Mates asserts.

Why Should We Do It?

We librarians are just so nice, we think information should be available to everyone. Right?

That's part of it, sure. But let's talk law and return on investment, here. We know that the Americans with Disabilities Act of 1990 (www.usdoj.gov/crt/ada/statute.html) means that public buildings must be reasonably accessible to all people.

In 2000, America Online settled a lawsuit brought against it by National Federation of the Blind. The suit took issue with AOL's Web browser, which was not compatible with screen-reader technology. The NFB was ready to prove that AOL was required to offer an accessible browser as part of a virtual "public accommodation" as per the ADA (Cisneros, Oscar S., "AOL Settles Accessibility Suit," *Wired News*, July 28, 2000, www.wired.com/news/business/0,1367,37845,00.html). In 2004, New York Attorney General Eliot Spitzer threatened legal action against Ramada.com and Priceline.com, claiming that their inaccessible Web sites violated the ADA. Both companies revamped their portals before suits could be filed.

Under Section 508 of the Rehabilitation Act as amended by Congress in 1998 (www.opm.gov/html/508-textOfLaw.asp), all

Federal agencies must ensure that any technology they employ must be accessible to employees and members of the public with disabilities. That includes Web pages. Anyone who sells to the Feds must comply with these standards, too.

Section 508: The Road to Accessibility
www.section508.gov

The U.S. General Services Administration designed this portal to help Federal agencies comply with Section 508 of the Rehabilitation Act, that is, to make their Web pages accessible to assistive technology users. The site has a lot of great information for anyone interested in inclusive Web page design. Especially look at the section called "508 Tools and Resources" (www.section508.gov/index. cfm?FuseAction=Content&ID=8) for links to accessibility information and software.

Legal imperatives for electronic accessibility can seem like a hassle. But it can also be a tremendous opportunity to prepare our electronic information for the future. An example: A Web page designed for inclusive use is probably also ready for on-the-fly conversion to Wireless Application Protocol, or WAP, devices. Those patrons who drive us crazy by talking on cell phones in the reference area? Soon they can search our catalogs on those things or on their PDAs. Imagine your patrons deep in the stacks, wireless catalog in their hands. No need to write anything down anymore. Fantasy? According to a national survey conducted for SBC in 2004, 19 percent of respondents owned a Web-enabled PDA (www.sbc.com/gen/press-room?pid=4800&cdvn=news&news articleid=21193). That number can only go up as mobile Web technology improves.

Wireless Google
www.google.com/wml

Point your cell phone browser to Wireless Google. Below the search box, select "Search Options." On the next screen, select the top choice: "Entire Web." Alternately, tab down to the "Go to URL" option. On the following screen, type in a search term or a URL, then press "Go." Note that URLs are case-sensitive and usually all lowercase. Google queries the entire 3-billion-plus-page universe of regular Web pages and then automatically translates the results, written in common HTML, into WML, the language that cell phones understand. The wee text browser on my mobile phone displays the Web as it appears to searchers using alternative technologies to access the Web. If I can't read it on my little phone (through the Google conversion service), they can't read it either.

Try viewing an accessible Web page, such as the Section 508 site mentioned earlier (www.section508.gov), on your phone through Wireless Google. It looks great! Who knew that inclusive Web page design would work so well on a telephone?

Accessible Web pages are also compatible with foreign language translators. According to Global Reach, a marketing research company, more than 64 percent of the world's Web users prefer to access the Internet by a language other than English (www. global-reach.biz/globstats/index.php3). When our pages translate easily, we broaden our audience considerably.

Almost one-fifth of our constituency considers themselves disabled in some way (www.census.gov/Press-Release/www/2002/cb02ff11.html). That number is expected to rise as the population ages. This is no "special interest group," but a substantial segment of the communities that we serve. They have a right to freedom of access to information and we librarians must help them exercise that right.

Finally, a library's outreach efforts can make awfully good press. For all these reasons, making our Web pages accessible is not only the law; it's a really good idea.

Temporarily Abled?

With everyone living so long, we all might consider ourselves merely "temporarily abled." If we live into our nineties, we must expect, accept, and plan for some loss of function. Our hearing will go and our sight, too. Our hands will tremble, making it hard for us to type and control a mouse. In short, we will *all* benefit from assistive technology one day, if we don't already.

Even the father of the Internet, Vint Cerf, has a hearing impairment. He emphasizes, "If you are deaf, you need captions for spoken elements. If you are blind, you need voiced descriptions of Web contents and spoken renderings of e-mail. The range of physical disabilities is very large, and we need many different tools to overcome the consequential barriers to Internet use" (www.pcworld.com/resource/article/0,aid,17690,pg,4,00.asp).

Judy Heim said, "Let us commit ourselves to truly assuring that the Internet really is for everyone" ("Locking Out the Disabled," *PC World*, September 1, 2000, www.pcworld.com/resource/article/0,aid,17690,pg,1,00.asp). Well put. And perfectly in line with our principles of librarianship. So, what are we waiting for? Let's get accessible!

Chapter 14

Computer Troubleshooting for Librarians

Imagine that libraries lend automobiles. Let's say we keep a fleet of a dozen or so. All the cars are economy models with sturdy pedigrees, such as Toyota or Honda, and all a couple of years old.

This is an extremely popular service at the library, so most of the cars are in use all day. Patrons sign up to use them at one-hour intervals. Driving skills vary widely among patrons. Some are savvy and do stunts in their cars. They complain that your cars don't go fast enough and may soup-up their rental with accessories and strange additives. Others have never driven before in their lives. "Excuse me. Where do you put in the key?" they ask. "How do you make it go?" They grind the gears and dent the fenders as they learn to drive in your parking lot—with your vehicles!

And we, the librarians, often man the front lines of responsibility for keeping these machines running smoothly. We ask ourselves, "Did I go to library school to become an auto mechanic? Have I just joined the pit-stop crew in the drag race of life?"

Now, instead of automobiles, think public access Internet terminals. Some days at the reference desk, I feel like I do nothing but baby-sit computers. "My computer froze!" "How do I send an attachment?" "Where's my print job?" my patrons cry. For major breakdowns, we call in our mechanics—that is, our computer guru guys. But for the little things that go wrong, we are on our own. And when we offer computer access to patrons, little things go wrong constantly.

We never expected to have to do this. Yet, helping patrons gain access to information means that we need knowledge of the *method* of access. In the case of the Internet, this means learning how to do at least minor troubleshooting on computers. With that in mind, let us roll up our sleeves, charge up our electric screwdrivers, and prepare to get our fingers dirty. Note that most of these tips are oriented toward personal computers using the Windows operating system, although some may work for Macintosh owners and Open Source users, too.

This sounds stupid, but if the computer doesn't turn on, you must check to see if the machine is plugged in properly and all the connections are tight. I called Dell Computer about a malfunctioning monitor a couple of years ago. This is when their computer help desk was in Texas, not Lahore. The first suggestion from the technician came in a thick Texas drawl: "Did you wiggle the wire?"

She had a point. The juncture of separable parts is the weak point in any circuit. Now, I always "wiggle the wire" on lifeless connections, trying to make the electrical juices flow once more.

I'm sure you know this, too: Before you begin to offer Internet access to anyone, public or staff, you must make certain that all your machines are equipped with both automatically updated anti-virus software and firewall software to help keep hackers from taking over your machines. The Internet is an essential tool in our work, but its unregulated nature makes even casual users vulnerable to nasty attacks.

Trend Micro Free Online Virus Scan
http://housecall.trendmicro.com

Do you wonder if your computer already has a virus? Trend Micro, makers of the anti-virus product PC-cillin, offers this free scan that will sense viruses lurking on your machine and eliminate them. This is no substitute for the constant vigilance provided by an up-to-date, real time virus-monitoring application installed on your PC. Think of it more as a "morning after" pill that compensates

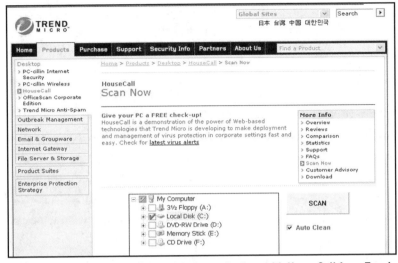

Figure 14.1   Scan your computer for viruses for free with HouseCall from Trend Micro.

for the indiscretion of allowing a computer to have unprotected access to the Internet.

Troubleshooting Tip One: Reboot

Our computer guru guy at the San Marino Public Library, Steve Lewis, is a computer repair genius. Sometimes he only has to walk into the room and the computers straighten up and begin working properly. It is as if he gives off an electronic aura that machines instinctively respect. If you ask Steve, "What is the first rule of computer troubleshooting?" he answers with one word: "Reboot."

"When someone calls me, the first question I ask is, 'Did you reboot?' I have seen it so many times," Lewis muses. "That solves the problem." Usually. Lewis cautions that, in certain cases, turning the computer off may cause you to lose data. Still, in most cases, on a Windows machine, rebooting just seems to help unscramble the computer's brains. You can try the "warm" boot, that is, asking Mr. Computer to cycle through its shutdown and restart procedures without shutting off its power. If Mr. C. is unresponsive, another variation of this maneuver involves delicately reaching over and jabbing the "reset" button on the front of the machine.

The "warm" boot didn't work? Try the "cold" boot: shutting down the machine completely, waiting two minutes, then turning it back on. You might even want to cut off the power at the surge protector. That gives all your peripheral devices (printers, etc.) a chance to reset themselves, too. This should do the trick. As with the "warm" boot, it is better if you can manage an orderly shutdown. Punching the power off suddenly may cause the reading device that skims just above the surface of the hard drive to plunge directly down into it, like a Concorde SST into a French hotel. The result could be disaster. Hard disk drive design has improved over the years, but the danger still exists. Remember, if you see the red "hard drive" light glowing on the face of your machine, don't just cut off the power. If that red light won't turn off, call your experts. If anyone's going to make any killer decisions here, let it be a techie.

Tip Two: Defrost Without Tears

One of my obsessive-compulsive-yet-learning-challenged patrons has done it again. She has opened so many Web pages with pop-up advertising windows that her browser finally gave up and froze. Do I have to turn the whole machine off to save the situation?

Maybe not. First, I will try that magical key combination, Control-Alt-Delete. Press the "Ctrl" key, then, while continuing to hold it down, press "Alt" and "Delete." When all three are down at once, a little window will appear on your screen that lists programs currently running. Select the one not working (in this case, the browser) then click on the "End Task" button. If you are lucky, closing that one frozen program should thaw the computer enough to get it working again.

If you are not lucky, simply press control-alt-delete again to perform a "warm" boot.

Interesting note: The code for Control-Alt-Delete was written by David J. Bradley in 1980 or '81 when he worked for IBM.

Other Secret Key Combinations for Windows

The secret of gaining a reputation as a computer genius lies in knowing a few simple tricks to amaze and confound your audience. In Windows, these secret tricks often consist of what are called "shortcut keys," combinations of keystrokes that accomplish what would otherwise involve pull-down menus and double clicks.

Let's say your mouse has stopped working. Press the "Ctrl" key, then "Esc." Control-escape will bring up your "Start" menu, allowing you to perform an orderly reboot. (By the way, so will the Windows key between the Ctrl and Alt keys on either side of the space bar on most keyboards.)

You've got two windows open. The window you want is hidden completely behind the other one. How do you get to it? Press "Alt" and "Tab" keys together to toggle to the window you used last.

Want to "Select All" of your document, "Copy" and "Paste" it somewhere else—without using a mouse? Type "Ctrl-A," "Ctrl-C," then "Ctrl-V." "Ctrl-C" and "Ctrl-V" are especially useful when no "Copy" or "Paste" commands appear on the toolbars of a program. Just because the programmers didn't choose to display these options does not mean that the Window-standard options won't work.

Got pop-ups, those annoying ads that appear in new browser windows over the pages you are trying to view? Press "Alt" and "F4" together to close them down.

Use these super shortcuts and I guarantee your clients will consider you a bona fide computer wizard. These are the commands that I use most, but there are certainly others. Search your "Windows Help" file (from the "Start" menu) for "shortcut keys." Or you might want to read one of those lucid and humorous "Dummies" books published by Wiley Publishing, Inc. (www.dummies.com), for example, *PCs For Dummies, 9th Edition* by Dan Gookin (2003, ISBN 0764540742). Visit the "Dummies" site to read helpful excerpts from that series.

Tip Three: Pound those Pop-ups

Speaking of pop-ups, who got the idea that annoying users with unwanted pop-up windows was a good way to sell things? Sometimes, pop-ups are a symptom of a computer infected with a virus or "spyware." Often though, pop-ups are simply advertising associated with a particular site. The site allows them because they gain advertising revenue. What they don't think about is that it makes users hate them. Although pop-up windows aren't as bad as malicious downloads, they can slow down computer performance and make surfing miserable.

Google Toolbar
http://toolbar.google.com

Although there are some fine programs that eliminate pop-ups, my favorite solution to this irritating problem is simply to install the Google toolbar for Internet Explorer and Mozilla's Firefox browser (www.mozilla.org/products/firefox). This petite addition to these browsers does a great job of eliminating most pop-up ads while allowing users who need a pop-up on a particular site to disable the feature with a click of the pop-up blocker icon. It also offers a search box that allows users to search the Web with Google from any site. Very handy.

Dogpile Search Toolbar
www.dogpile.com/info.dogpl/tbar

InfoSpace's metasearch engine Dogpile now comes as a toolbar that has the same pop-up blocking power as Google's. Plus, it allows users to pull in RSS feeds that scroll across as a ticker on its search bar all day long. This toolbar works only with Internet Explorer.

Tip Four: Slash that Spyware and Mash that Malware

"Can I ask you something?" asks a wraithlike user who haunts our public access stations. "When the flashing banner on the screen says that I am a lucky winner and that I should click 'OK' to claim my prize, should I do it?"

It's not a stupid question. After all, how many of our computer users can resist redeeming a reward or accepting a free scan to help the computer run faster? Yet, these advertising banners are not what they appear to be. They *never* deliver the promised premium. Instead, they download harmful programs onto our computers. Called "spyware," this software is designed to harvest computer information and send it back to the advertiser for its own use. Doxdesk.com blogger Andrew Clover calls this class of program "unsolicited commercial software."

This tactic is technically legal because users must click on an "OK" button before the program is installed. Unfortunately, because the explanation of the download is purposefully misleading, most users are not aware that this consent opens their computer to outside forces that may track their online behavior, download unlimited advertising to their browser, or even change their home page to one of the advertiser's choosing. (This is especially troublesome when the hijacked home page points to a pornographic site.)

In some cases, spyware downloads itself automatically when users visit certain Web sites. This kind of attack is called a "drive-by download." Just as it is wise for most citizens to avoid urban areas where there is gang activity, security-minded computer-users may want to steer clear of Web neighborhoods featuring arcade games and video game cheats, LyricsDomain (that offers free song lyrics), any "free" pornography, and, oddly, sites about wrestling.

Not only that, but spyware and "malware" (software specifically designed to harm a computer) is often poorly written and tends to suck up a computer's processing power.

A National Cyber Security Alliance (NCSA) survey conducted in October 2004 found that 80 percent of home computers harbor spyware and adware, but that 88 percent of users did not realize that they were infected (www.staysafeonline.info/pdf/safety_study_v04.pdf).

What to do about this disturbing problem? First, make certain that your Windows-based computer is up-to-date with all the patches put out by its parent company, Microsoft. Windows is a product that is always evolving, struggling to patch holes that bad guys find in its security. To find the latest updates, open the Internet Explorer browser. Pull down the "Tools" menu on the top bar and click "Windows Updates." This will take you to the Windows update page at Microsoft (http://windowsupdate.micro soft.com). Let the site scan your computer for the updates that you need, then let it install them for you. Users of Windows XP and later versions of Windows can request that important updates download and install themselves automatically. Do this by clicking on the "System" folder in the Control Panel on the computer. One of the tabs will read "Automatic Updates." This display lets you choose your download schedule. When the "update icon" appears near the time on the lower right corner of your desktop, it means that an update is ready to install. Click on the icon, a picture of a globe with a Microsoft flag over its upper left quadrant, to install the update.

Macintosh users may update their operating systems, too, although Apples are known for being invulnerable to spyware. On Mac OSX or later, the "Software Update" program resides in "System Preferences," located on the Apple pull-down menu. On earlier Macs, the "Software Update" program is in the "Control Panel." All versions can be set to download software updates automatically.

Technically-savvy Windows XP users can use the Control-Alt-Delete key combination to invoke the task manager to see what rogue process might be running. Most of us though are not experts at deciphering Windows process names. I mean, is "lsass.exe" a good thing or a bad thing?

Task List Programs
www.answersthatwork.com/Tasklist_pages/tasklist.htm

We don't want to remove the wrong process and crash our computers completely. So, we will want to check suspicious process names against the alpha list of Windows task descriptions at AnswersThatWork (www.answersthatwork.com). Turns out, C:\Windows\System32\LSASS.exe is an integral part of the operating system. Best not remove that one.

For those of us who don't want to pluck out possible spyware by hand, there are these online services to help us eliminate spyware from our computers.

TrendMicro Spyware Scan
www.trendmicro.com/spyware-scan/

Trend Micro Anti-Spyware for the Web is a free online tool that checks computers for spyware, and helps remove any infections found. When the detection process is complete, the tool will display a report describing the result including which, if any, spyware were detected, and prompt you before the removal process.

SpywareInfo Online Spyware Detection
www.spywareinfo.com/xscan.php

SpywareInfo and XBlock (www.xblock.com), maker of X-Cleaner Spyware Remover, join forces to offer this Web-based application. It scans for all supported "adwares" and many of the "spywares," keyloggers, and trojans that the downloadable freeware version of X-Cleaner also targets. Works best from Internet Explorer.

Spyaudit
www.webroot.com/services/spyaudit_03.htm

Webroot offers this free program that scans your system registry and hard drive space for thousands of known spyware programs. Although Spy Audit displays the spyware that is on your system, it does not remove any files.

eTrust PestScan
www.ca.com/products/pestpatrol

Visit the "Spyware Center" at Computer Associates' "CA Security Advisor Site" to get a free online spyware scan of your computer. Because it uses Active X controls, this online scan only works with Internet Explorer. It finds a lot of spyware, but this free scan does not remove it.

According to a study conducted by Eric Howe of the University of Illinois Urbana-Champaign in late 2004 (http://spywarewarrior. com/asw-test-guide.htm), no spyware removal product used alone removes much more than 50 percent of known spyware.

It turns out that spyware is like cancer: It is best controlled by using multiple attacks at the same time. Remember that there are fake spy removal programs out there, many of which install rather than remove offending software. The following programs are proven safe and effective against spyware. Many are free; the rest are cheap. Download at least three of them and run them one after the other.

Before you use the following products, it helps to reboot into "Safe Mode." Here's how. Restart your computer. As it boots, before Windows loads, press the F8 key a few times. You will see a screen that offers a variety of boot options. Choose to boot in the Safe Mode with networking. Now when Windows starts, it will only have its most basic programs running—not the spyware. This allows your spyware removal tools to operate swiftly, without interference. You will still have access to the Internet so you can download the latest spyware definitions.

After you have run your spyware removal programs, reboot normally. With any luck, you will be spyware free!

Ad-Aware
http://lavasoft.element5.com/default.shtml.en

Sweden's Lavasoft has fought spyware for years with its Ad-Aware program. Ad-Aware scans the hard drive for rogue registry entries and tracking files then eliminates them. This reliable program is available in three levels of protection. The "Professional" version provides the most protection and can be implemented over a network. Ad-Aware Plus updates itself and is good for smaller implementations. The "personal edition" remains free for noncommercial use.

Spybot S&D (Search and Destroy)
www.safer-networking.org/en/home/index.html

Romantic German programmer Patrick M. Kolla, who dedicates his work "to the most wonderful girl on earth :)," gives us this free program. It makes a good complement to Ad-Aware (mentioned above) as it often catches spyware that the other misses. It also "immunizes" the computer against many major spyware products. Although Kolla offers his program gratis, be sure to send him some cash to thank him for his work.

CWShredder
www.intermute.com/products/cwshredder.html

There is a particular kind of spyware that is very difficult to remove called CoolWebSearch. Its code changes constantly, but it invariably redirects users to coolwebsearch.com and its affiliates. (Tip: Don't visit that site to check. It might download itself as a "drive-by.") The malware changes your home page, adds links to porn sites, and inserts a toolbar into Internet Explorer. It also slows down your PC and makes it very unstable, causing it to crash and reboot randomly.

The only way to get CoolWebSearch off of a PC is to run CWShredder. This free program was developed and maintained as a public service by Merijn Bellekom of the Netherlands. It has recently been purchased and is now maintained by it new owner, Trend Micro.

Spy Sweeper
www.webroot.com

Webroot offers this powerful spyware removal tool for about $30 per year.

HijackThis: Merijn.org
www.spywareinfo.com/~merijn/downloads.html

Merijn Bellekom, the same fellow from the Netherlands who wrote CWShredder, also developed this downloadable program that examines and displays files on key areas of the hard drive, particularly the Registry. Most of the files on the list will be legitimate, but some may be spyware. Users may delete suspect files themselves, but HijackThis offers the option to copy the list of files onto a support group bulletin board, for example the "TomCoyote Forum" for "HijackThis Logs and Spyware/Malware Removal" (http://forums.tomcoyote.org/). There, eager volunteer experts guide rookie users about what files should stay and what can be thrown out. Mr. Bellekom offers other handy freeware programs on his site, too.

Microsoft Windows Anti-Spyware (Beta)
www.microsoft.com/athome/security/spyware/software/
default.mspx

Microsoft recently purchased Giant AntiSpyware, a very good spyware removal tool. It offers it now to Windows XP users as a free beta-test product, at least to the end of 2005. Although it catches some things, it ignores the Gator products from Claria.com and the "iWon" suite of spyware. It has "delisted" these as threats because it now sees them as benign advertisers, not malicious computer-wreckers and privacy-invaders.

How can we keep this spyware from coming down on our computers in the first place?

One way for Windows users to discourage spyware is to eschew Internet Explorer for "alternative" browsers such as Opera (http://www.opera.com) and Mozilla's Firefox (www.mozilla.org/products/firefox). The free version of Opera sports has an ad-banner, but that disappears for the subscription price of about $80 per year. Firefox, based on the original browser behind Netscape, is not only free, but based upon source software, so it is constantly being updated by volunteers as well as its own company.

This is not a foolproof technique. Attackers have found vulnerabilities that allow them to work through Firefox to exploit weaknesses in Internet Explorer! Still, if you and your family keep all your browsers updated and generally use the alternative ones, your risk of downloading spyware is reduced.

SpywareBlaster
www.javacoolsoftware.com/spywareblaster.html

Here is a program that "prevents the installation of ActiveX-based spyware, adware, dialers, browser-hijackers, and other malware or potentially unwanted programs," according to its Web site. It is free for personal and educational use, although the company accepts donations for its good work. Automatically updated spyware definitions are available for just $10 per year per computer. Definitely worth it.

IE-SPYAD

http://netfiles.uiuc.edu/ehowes/www/resource.htm

This application keeps spyware from installing itself. Eric L. Howes teaches business and technical writing at the University of Illinois at Urbana-Champaign. Yet, he is also a fearless crusader against the spyware and malware that are the bane of Web use today. He offers great tips and links about removing these stealthy parasites from computers. He has even written a free downloadable application, IE-SPYAD, to "stop unwanted crapware from being installed behind your back via 'drive-by-downloads'." It works with the Internet Explorer browser.

Home PC Firewall Guide

www.firewallguide.com

Spyware prevention is just one part of the security suite needed to protect every Windows computer connected to the Internet. It's all so complicated that most of us would rather ignore the whole thing. What anti-virus program should I buy? What is a firewall, exactly? Visit this site to find clear, current explanations of home computer network security issues and what to do about them.

Spyware Info

www.spywareinfo.com

Wily, unscrupulous marketers are always coming up with new ways to sell us things—and mess up our computers. Writer and software consultant Mike Healan offers explanations of spyware along with "the tools and knowledge you need to protect your privacy from the onslaught of spyware, adware, and corporate and government surveillance." He hosts support forums and a chat room in which users can exchange tips. Healan also publishes his Spyware Weekly Newsletter. Read it online, subscribe to it via e-mail (www.spywareinfo.com/subscribe), or pick up the RSS feed with your favorite aggregator.

Spyware Guide
www.spywareguide.com

Foster City, California's FaceTime Communications, brings us this Spyware Guide offering links to anti-spyware software and also to lists of companies distributing spyware as well as software and applications known to contain spyware. "As the spy versus spy battle rages on we have decided to document this fascinating battlefield," states the Web site. Subscribe to its "SpywareGuide Update List" via e-mail, or pick up the RSS feed.

Ben Edelman
www.benedelman.org

Edelman is a PhD candidate at Harvard who is studying the methods and effects of spyware, with a focus on installation methods and revenue sources. That is, whose investment money is paying for all that advertising spyware out there? Edelman knows, and he's telling.

Doxdesk.com
www.doxdesk.com

Andrew Clover blogs about the latest news in the evil spyware universe. He offers tips about what to do about it.

Tip Five: Scandisk and Defrag

These two system utilities from Microsoft help users maintain file systems on their Windows operating systems. (The Macintosh utility that scans and defrags is known as "Disk First Aid.") Windows keeps track of the location of the files on the hard drive with a kind of table of contents called the File Allocation Table (FAT for short—except on Windows 2000 and XP, where it becomes the Master File Table, aka MFT). When you add or delete a lot of material, the FAT can get out-of-date.

To fix this problem on Windows 9x machines, run the ScanDisk program located under Programs/Accessories/System Tools. It will rewrite the File Allocation Table to reflect the current state of the hard drive. On XP and later, this utility is called "Chkdsk" or Check Disk. In "My Computer" or "Windows Explorer," right-click the drive you want to check and then click "Properties." Under the "Tools" tab, click "Check Now." There you go.

Over time, as you delete files, empty spaces form on the hard drive. Newly added material interfiles itself in the various lacunae, spreading itself all over the drive. You can imagine that it takes the computer longer than it should to run a program when it has to skip all over the place to get at all the information it needs. Fix this problem by running the defragmentation utility ("defrag" to its friends) to co-locate files on the hard drive.

It does a librarian's heart good to see defrag at work. The application combs the hard drive and pulls all the files together in good order. Caution: Don't run it when you need to finish a rush job. Defrag can take hours to complete. On Windows 2000, defrag can only work on a reboot, a disadvantage if you don't have hours to kill before you get down to work or if this computer has to do duty as a 24/7 Internet server.

Windows NT doesn't even come with a defrag utility. For systems based on this operating system, you should buy a commercial product, such as Executive Software International's Diskeeper (www.executive.com/diskeeper/diskeeper.asp) or Syman-tec's Norton Systemworks (www.symantec.com/sabu/sysworks/basic) to get the job done.

On your hard-driven public access computers, you will want to run these utilities about once a week. They will keep your machines operating at peak performance and perhaps prevent future system crashes.

Tip Six: Erase the Damage

Several programs exist that can erase changes that users make to public access computers. No matter what the patron does—

erase files, install software, download viruses or spyware, or tamper with desktop settings—these applications will rollback the machines to a previous pristine configuration upon restart. When the programs work well, they eliminate most of the futzing with fixing. Because reboot/restore utilities also eliminate all history settings, logs, and temporary files, they are valuable for preserving the privacy of our public access users.

Deep Freeze
www.faronics.com

The granddaddy of reboot/restore utilities, this software is easy to deploy and works very well, especially on XP machines. It allows computer administrators to designate a portion of the drive as a nonerase zone. Simply map files such as usage statistics to this drive so they will persist over reboot/restore cycles.

Other products that restore a clean image on reboot include Clean Slate from Fortres Grand Corporation (www.fortres. com/products/cleanslate.htm), Driveshield from Centurion Technologies (www.centurionguard.com), and Drive Vaccine (www.horizondatasys.com/drivevaccine/index.html) which works with both PCs and Macintosh workstations.

Another option is to make an exact copy or "image" of a pristine computer configuration. When the computer gets so messed it up that it can no longer easily be fixed, you can use this image to restore a nice clean hard drive.

Norton Ghost
www.symantec.com/sabu/ghost/ghost_personal

Designed to back up personal hard drives, this program is easily adapted to the purpose of restoring a public access system that has become irrevocably twisted.

Figure 14.2　Deep Freeze restores public access computers to their original state upon reboot.

Tip Seven: Use Soap and Water

Now that you've cleaned up your files, it is time to wash the computer itself. One of the best things you can do for the poor thing is take a can of pressurized air and clean out the fan on the back of the CPU. Go ahead. Take a look at that fan right now. It is absolutely covered in crud, right? No wonder the computer sounds like an airplane taking off. Cleaning off the fan is almost like changing the oil in your car. It helps your machine run cool and smooth.

While you're at it, clean the mouse. It can get very dirty, with oils from many hands mixed with the dust of days. New laser-based mice respond nicely to a quick rubdown with cloth damp with mild cleansers. Older trackball-based mice require more detailed cleaning. Turn the mouse over and open the cover over the mouse ball. Use your compressed air to blow fuzz out of the chamber. Put rubbing alcohol on a cotton swab to carefully clean the gunk off the rollers around the ball. Be careful not to leave pieces of cotton swab inside the mouse. Replace the ball and its cover. The mouse should return to its old, responsive self.

You can clean the keyboard, too. First, use the compressed air to spray the big bits out from under the keys. Then, spray ammonia-based window cleaner on a cloth or rag and use this damp cloth to wipe the key tops. You probably want to do this when the machine is off to prevent accidental commands going to the CPU. You might even want to wipe the keys with a bit of antibacterial solution. Let's face it: Not all viruses around a public computer occur inside the computer; people pass disease around with their hands. After a day of public pawing, those keyboards must be crawling. BTW, where are my surgeon gloves?

You can use tweezers or needle-nosed pliers to pry off individual keys to clean under them. I even heard about someone who successfully ran a filthy keyboard through the dishwasher, but I'm not recommending that. The best bet is to keep people with food and drink far away from your computers. As Jeff Davis of ZDNet has written, "It's almost a rule in the computer industry: Half-filled cups of coffee left on computer components will eventually spill."

Where to Find More Help

After I restore an image or bring to fore a lost window, my awed patrons often ask, "Where did you learn how to do all this with computers?" I twist my mouth and respond wryly, "Bitter experience, my dears."

With computers, as with love, nothing smoothes the path more than having traveled the road at least once before. How many hours have I wasted cussing at my recalcitrant machine? It certainly helps to get a little guidance from others. Sometimes, just a word in your ear can steer you in the right direction. Here are some resources that can help.

Web4Lib Electronic Discussion
http://lists.webjunction,org/web4lib

Roy Tennant and his comrades at the UC Berkeley Library have managed this searchable list that stretches back to 1994. Comb the collected knowledge of your fellow digital information professionals to find out what others do to solve the same problems that you face. This site really is the source of all knowledge for digital librarians. You can even use this site to find yourself a new job.

Microsoft Help and Support
http://support.microsoft.com

Get Windows help straight from the horse's mouth on this site. Search the Knowledge Base for an article relevant to your trouble. Or, look into the Product Support Centers for answers to FAQs (frequently asked questions) categorized by product.

Annoyances.org
http://annoyances.org

"Annoyances.org is the most complete collection of information assembled for and by actual users of Microsoft Windows." This site,

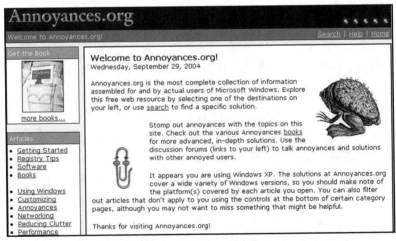

Figure 14.3   Find out how to get around those Windows annoyances at Annoyances.org.

from Creative Element (www.creativelement.com), is free, searchable, and covers all versions of Windows. Very useful.

Windows Support Center
http://aumha.org

James A. Eshelman offers free help for Windows users of all stripes. He includes links to useful freeware available on the Web. He even includes online lessons in HTML. What a guy!

PC Help Mobile
http://ralphcaddell.com/pchelp

Chemical Engineer Ralph Caddell owns and operates Mobile, Alabama's Computer Help Site. His friendly instructions can help any Windows-based librarian/*de facto* computer technician work through most common problems.

PCWorld
www.pcworld.com

This online version of the popular technology magazine offers a "Tips & Troubleshooting" section for help with common PC complaints.

Optimize XP
http://mywebpages.comcast.net/SupportCD/OptimizeXP.html

Mysterious Andrew K., a full-time technical service manager, has gathered a bunch of links to very helpful programs to help keep Windows XP systems running strong. His annotations and instructions are clear and he keeps his collection current.

Extreme Tech
www.extremetech.com

Ziff Davis Publishing Holdings, Inc. brings us Extreme Tech, a site that offers analysis and tutorials for many computing issues. For example, when I had trouble connecting to my broadband connection via Windows XP, I visited their "Windows XP Roundup," featuring a series of articles detailing bugs and other issues in the news with this operating system. Find info by typing keywords into the search box at the very top of the page. This site says that it offers "deep technology for enthusiasts and professionals." Hey! They left out "librarians"!

Information Professional or Free Support Desk?

One minute you are cheerfully helping patrons navigate the Web in the library, and the next they are calling you from home for help with their Internet accounts. Should you help these folks?

Absolutely yes, writes Sara Weissman, head of Electronic Reference at the Morris County Library in Whippany, New Jersey. "Don't turn them away," she writes. "Being the mediators of the Internet for the patron is great publicity and good will for the library. We can't tout Internet access in our libraries while denying we know how to use it when patrons have problems" ("Shoptalk," *NetConnect*, supplement to *Library Journal*, October 15, 1999).

Weissman suggests creating a standardized checklist of what your staff will and won't do. What are you responsible for? Most likely, support for your catalog, Web site, and access to your remote vendors. Train the reference staff in troubleshooting your products and give them a cheat-sheet so that everyone gives the same advice, referrals, and examples.

"You are not responsible for the fix, necessarily," notes Weissman, "just for listening and responding. Thank them for reporting the problem! They feel useful and it eases frustration."

Computer Rage and Limits

On the other hand, Laurie Van Court, reference librarian at the P. S. Miller Library in Castle Rock, Colorado, sent me an e-mail recently asking about the problem of "techno-jerks." "These are the guys (yes, mostly guys) who already know everything there is to know about computers. When they have problems on our computers, it is always the fault of our systems, solvable only by the HEAD OF TECHNOLOGY. (Right now, of course, if not sooner.) Mere reference librarians are never competent enough for these guys"(from a private e-mail).

When I was single, I wore makeup when I went to the laundromat with the idea that I might meet a potential mate there. What I forgot was, if a man is in the laundromat in the middle of a weekday, he a) probably doesn't have a job, and b) is not independently wealthy enough to buy his own washing machine. These factors may indicate that this person has adjustment problems that would affect all aspects of his life and make him a less than ideal partner. (*I* was an artiste at the time—I had an excuse. Or maybe not.)

I feel the same today about the gentlemen who spend their days at our computer terminals. If many among them suffer mild mental illness, we can accommodate that as a disability. But we should not tolerate disdain or abuse from Internet patrons. If a male techno-jerk considers a female reference librarian inadequate to solve his computer problems, he needs to be made aware of a few library realities.

First of all, using computers in the library is a privilege, not a right.

Secondly, we will *never* have enough computers and we aren't going to get any more any time soon.

Third, our equipment will always be outdated.

We help our patrons to access information on the Web and we may enhance our service with handouts, fairly clear interfaces, and staff training. Still, we are not Kinkos. We do not offer all-purpose publishing and Internet services. If a cranky patron doesn't like our computer facilities, he is free to go pay to use someone else's.

The problem comes when the customers get nasty. Staff has to work as a unit to manage troublesome patron behaviors. Tough to do, though. Especially since library workers live to help and can get discombobulated when patrons disrespect our abilities.

I have found solace in a phrase described by Susan Berk, library consultant, as "step back" language. She advises establishing a link with the angry patron by saying, "I understand you." But then she continues with the next component of her script, "I am required to adhere to library policy" (From Berk's workshop about problem patrons given at the Cerritos Library on May 15, 2003). That phrase, "I am required," takes the disagreement out of the realm of the personal. We are *all* required to adhere to library policy. So, no arguing. Our patrons agree to our rules when they sit down at our computer. Like rowdy bar flies, they can be shown the door if they get too obnoxious.

Now You Know Everything

Fooled you, didn't I? We both know I have merely scratched the surface of the complicated business of running public access computers. Notice that I haven't even touched the issue of the queuing or time-out software that helps with computer crowd control. Still, I hope that these tips help you through some common sticky situations with those irritating yet essential machines we work with every day. Ours is a service profession, and provide service we must—mechanical as well as intellectual.

Chapter 15

Keeping Up with Changes on the Web

"Dang!" my son hollers at the TV. He's playing a video game called "Sponge Bob Squarepants: Battle for Bikini Bottom." He is frustrated because the evil villain Prawn is attacking him not only with lethal sonic waves but also with robots, ever growing numbers of robots.

"How am I supposed to jump over the beams when I keep getting attacked by so many stinking robots?!" he wails.

Do you ever feel, with this whole Internet thing, like someone just sat you down in front of a video game that you've never seen before and expected you to leap every sonic wave that comes your way? Or maybe you've just managed to catch the rhythm of the lethal beams and some fiend sends an army of robots to attack you at the same time?

How in the heck are we supposed to keep up with changes on the Web? Some of us have *jobs*. We can't just sit around playing on the Net all day like it was some video game, even if we wanted to.

Fear not, friends. Plenty of free current awareness services exist out there, dedicated to bringing you early warning of incoming Web resources. Jump! Here comes another killer bunch!

New Site Locators

New sites come at you, faster than you can count them. How can you tell which are important? Here are some services that will help you sort out new sites on the Web.

Librarians' Index to the Internet:
New This Week Mailing List and RSS Feed
http://lii.org/search/file/mailinglist

Sign up for LII's current awareness service for keeping track of great new Web sites. At about 10 A.M. on Thursday morning, the Librarians' Index to the Internet will e-mail you a list of the best 10 to 20 Web sites newly added to this high-quality, searchable resource. Alternatively, you can subscribe to their RSS feed, which delivers the same information to an "aggregator" Web site. (See their "What the Heck Is RSS?" explanation at http://lii.org/search/file/liirss.)

Yahoo! What's New
http://dir.yahoo.com/new

Get the scoop on new, handpicked sites added to Yahoo! in the last week. Or, sign up for the Yahoo! Daily Wire, an e-mail that points out three new and noteworthy Web sites, a Yahoo! Pick, and plenty of links to interesting starting points.

Forbes.com: Best of the Web
www.forbes.com/bow

Every quarter, the editors at Forbes.com select and analyze Web sites that support the lifestyle to which we *wish* we were all accustomed. Browse categories such as Collecting, Investing, Education, Travel, Luxe Shopping, and The Good Life. If we can surf it, we can live it.

Neat New Stuff I Found on the Net This Week
http://marylaine.com/neatnew.html

Don't be daunted by Iowa-based Marylaine Block's quaint turns of phrase. She's as current a cybrarian as they come. Every week she scours the Web for sites useful to librarians then wraps them up in a "neat" package. Subscribe to her e-mail bulletins at her site.

El Dorado County Library: What's Hot on the Internet This Week
www.eldoradolibrary.org/thisweek.htm

Think "Gold Country." Gary Parks of the Placerville, California, El Dorado County Library pans the fast-flowing Web every week.

Figure 15.1   Surf the good life at Forbes.com Best of the Web.

Read his assays of the precious resources he has discovered over the last four months. He covers sites of local interest to those living near Sacramento as well as fine national and international Web pages.

Free Pint

www.freepint.com/index.html

Need a British perspective on the ever-changing Web? Belly up to the bar and get your Free Pint, a fortnightly newsletter written by "information professionals who share how they find quality and reliable information on the Internet." Alternately, subscribe to the Bar Digest, which consists of the latest postings from the Free Pint Bar delivered to your e-mail inbox twice a week, all in return for free registration. The Free Pint Bar is also available as an RSS feed at http://web.freepint.com/library/broadcast_freepint_bar.xml.

Beyond the Black Stump
http://home.mira.net/~lions/pppowww.htm

Aussie computer dude "Pirate Pete" Garriga puts a down-under spin on the latest sites, demonstrating once again why we call it the *World* Wide Web. "Beyond the Black Stump" is Australian for "way out in the boondocks." Sign up for the weekly Blackstump newsletter to learn about cool Web pages, Australiana, and more.

New Hardware and Software

When the Web was born, the hard part for me was not the myriad resources available, it was the fact that I needed to use computers to get to them. I'm a librarian, not a computer technician. Even if we learn how to use what we have, it keeps changing, morphing into unfamiliar forms. The following sites can help us keep on top of new technology.

The Library Web Manager's Reference Center
http://lists.webjunction.org/web4lib/faq.html

Confused about technology and don't know where to start looking for help? Before you do anything, click over to the Web4Lib Reference Center. It is packed with links to quality Web resources that will tell you how to connect your library to the Web, help you with Web authoring and site management, advise you on public access issues and software, and offer hints on how to organize the Internet. Maintained by Jennifer Ward, this site culls information from the Web4Lib electronic discussion list (http://sunsite3.berkeley.edu/Web4Lib).

The Shifted Librarian
www.theshiftedlibrarian.com

"Jenny Levine has one simple goal," writes *Library Journal* in its March 15, 2003 issue. "To help us librarians become as technologically adept as our users are so that we can deliver services to them when and where they wish to use them and in their preferred medium and platform." In other words, she checks out gadgets and tells us how we can use them in our work. With Jenny's help, we librarians don't have to be perpetually in the dark about new stuff. Feed her RSS to your aggregator.

Figure 15.2   Jenny Levine helps librarians get more comfortable with technology.

The Harrow Technology Report
www.theharrowgroup.com/index.htm

Jeffrey R. Harrow writes this weekly newsletter about advances in computer technology. Read it on the site, or sign up for automatic e-mail delivery. This newsletter was formerly known as The Rapidly Changing Face of Computing.

Library Stuff
www.librarystuff.net

Steven M. Cohen maintains this library Weblog dedicated to helping librarians keep up with changing technology. Read his blog or subscribe to his RSS feed.

Current Cites

http://lists.webjunction.org/currentcites

Roy Tennant and company produce this electronic publication that abstracts important new articles relevant to information technology. Subscribe to its listserve to receive this monthly newsletter electronically.

TechnoBiblio

www.technobiblio.com

Designed and maintained by Stephanie Wright and Aaron Smith, this site discusses new technologies that can impact and improve libraries. Its motto: "Where librarians and technogeeks speak the same language." Of course you can get its content delivered to your aggregator Web site via RSS. I'm surprised you even had to ask.

ResourceShelf

www.resourceshelf.com

Never fear, librarians! Gary Price is here with all the information news that's fit to blog. Or, get his daily newsletter sent to your e-mail. Or better yet, just pick up his RSS feed.

Computer and Business News

Find out where the real action is—in the interplay between money and machines—from these sites.

New York Times: Technology

www.nytimes.com/pages/technology/index.html

Free registration gains you access to all the Web news fit to print—or post on the Web. The "CyberTimes" section of this site offers daily articles covering e-commerce, education, and cyber law. Look to the David Pogue's "Circuits" column for news from the human side of the Web. And the whole thing is searchable. Sign up to get the headlines e-mailed directly to you, or subscribe via RSS.

Los Angeles Times: Cutting Edge
www.latimes.com/technology

The paper's technology section, a subset of its business coverage, looks at the ways computers are changing—and changing our lives.

CNN.com: Technology
www.cnn.com/TECH

This site covers "the big picture"—not so much the Web itself, but the Web as it interacts with social trends, cell phones, and the shrinking polar cap. Visit this site to get a sense of the technology trends of tomorrow or subscribe to their newsletter and have the trends visit you.

USA Today: Tech
www.usatoday.com/tech/front.htm

Get the overview of what is happening in the computer/business world, including a snapshot of what's cool on the Internet in "Web Guide" (www.usatoday.com/tech/webguide/front.htm)

BusinessWeek Online: Technology
www.businessweek.com/technology

Joan Frye-Williams, technical planning consultant for libraries, revealed this hot tip in one of her workshops: "Read this section every week. It is written for busy managers who aren't tech gurus with an eye to keeping them informed about what new technology will help their businesses" (from a personal conversation). Williams asserts that information professionals can also stay abreast of helpful new technologies by investing 15 minutes per week reading these stories.

Slashdot: News for Nerds. Stuff that Matters
http://slashdot.org

I actually like Slashdot a lot, although the computer argot used here puts much of the discussion beyond my absolute comprehension. Still, I keep a link on my "personal toolbar" and check in

Figure 15.3   Read tech news written for non-techie managers at BusinessWeek Online.

with the site about once a week. I almost always find out something new, interesting, and important about technology.

Wired News

www.wired.com/news

It's almost too hip—yet still useful. Visit Wired News to get the latest on the continuing digital revolution and analysis of the Information Age technologies.

ResearchBuzz

www.researchbuzz.com

Tara Calishain, site queen and author of the bestselling book *Google Hacks* (O'Reilly, 2003, ISBN 0596004478), writes, "ResearchBuzz is designed to cover the world of Internet research. To that end this site provides almost daily updates on search engines, new data managing software, browser technology, large compendiums of information, Web directories—whatever. If in doubt, the final question is, 'Would a reference librarian find it useful?' If the answer's yes, in it goes!" Read her site or have her entertaining newsletter e-mailed to you weekly. Need more? Pay $30 per year for ReseachBuzz Extra.

URLwire

www.urlwire.com/headlines

Eric Ward handpicks the stories, writes the annotations, and sends the news only to those people who write about the Internet every day. He breaks the big Web stories. Read his stuff here or pick up his RSS feed.

Subject-Specific Web Resources

Whether your interests lie in business or academics, explore these resources to find the latest in specific subject areas.

ALA: Internet Resources

www.ala.org/ala/acrl/acrlpubs/crlnews/internetresources.htm

It's academic, no question. With topics like "Information Architecture" and "East Asian Studies," these monthly resource guides read like descriptions in a college catalog. But what else would you expect from the Association of College and Research Libraries (ACRL)? Browse the subject reviews in chronological or alphabetical order.

Blue Web'n

www.kn.pacbell.com/wired/bluewebn

This searchable database connects to at least 1,000 outstanding Web sites relevant to children and school. Resources are categorized by subject area, audience, and type, for example, lessons, activities, projects, and references. Subscribe to the "Blue Web'n Weekly Update" to get a weekly e-mail of the Hot Site of the Week and new Blue Web'n sites. This service is sponsored by SBC, a California-based telephone company.

LLRX.com: Legal and Technology Articles and Resources for Librarians, Lawyers, and Law Firms
www.llrx.com

Editor Sabrina I. Pacifici offers news and site reviews of interest to legal researchers. For law and technology news, updated weekdays, visit Pacifici's blog, beSpacific.com (www.bespacific.com), or have its info e-mailed to you. LLRX.com is also available as an RSS feed.

Connie Crosby: Info Diva
http://conniecrosby.blogspot.com

Connie Crosby, a law librarian from Canada, keeps us up-to-date on mostly Canadian-oriented Web resources. Pull her feed onto your RSS aggregator site.

Useit.com: Jakob Nielsen's Web Site
www.useit.com

Dr. Jakob Nielsen has harangued the Web world with diatribes about the necessity for useable Web design since 1995. Although the body of his work is infused with irritability, he still gives a lot of good advice. His Web site gives all kinds of news—and his opinions—about the latest in Web technology and site design. Sign up to receive alerts by e-mail when Nielsen's articles are published.

Search Engine Watch
www.searchenginewatch.com

Trust Danny Sullivan to bring you the latest headlines about Web searching and search engines. Read his monthly Search Engine Report for free or subscribe for more in-depth information at the site for $99 per year. Sullivan's reports are also available via RSS feed.

SearchDay Newsletter
www.searchenginewatch.com/searchday

Chris Sherman, associate editor of the aforementioned Search Engine Watch, keeps users informed about Web-searching trends in a friendly, companionable way. Read his daily column on the

Web or have it pushed to your inbox. Sign up at http://search enginewatch.com/sereport.

Print-Plus Resources

Maybe you don't want your news delivered digitally. Maybe sometimes you'd just like to settle back with a hand full of print and a hot cup of joe. If you prefer your Web news in hard copy, try these resources.

Information Today, Inc.
www.infotoday.com

Excellent. You spotted the conflict of interest. Information Today, Inc. is the publisher of this book. Nonetheless, Information Today also publishes a fine array of current periodicals, all designed to keep users and producers of information products and services up to speed. You can also order books or subscribe to periodicals, such as *Information Today, Computers in Libraries, Online,* and, yes, *Searcher,* online. Also, Information Today's Web site offers Newsbreaks (www.infotoday.com/newsbreaks) about important happenings in the electronic information world, along with a free e-zine, NewsLink, which will push news to your inbox.

INFO TO GO: Navigating the Internet
www.infotogo.com

Irvine, California-based Info to Go is dedicated "to eliminating aimless surfing!" Their "highly selective" monthly newsletter features coverage of subject-area gateways as well as the latest Internet resources, tools, and news. A sampling of their material appears on their blog (www.infotogo.blogspot.com).

The Charleston Advisor
www.charlestonco.com

This quarterly publication serves the serious consumer of electronic resources on the Internet. Subscribe to this publication for industrial-strength reviews with objective and reliable critical evaluations. Go to their site to sign up.

Keeping Up—With Your Mail!

Enough, already! Now, you have so much current awareness information coming at you that you won't be able to keep track of it. Talk about information overload!

Your best bet is to pick a few of these services that best suit your needs. After all, nobody can keep track of everything. If you discover even a handful of resources that will serve you and your patrons, you will seem like an omniscient genius—a genius that can juggle robots and jump deadly beams at the same time, with the press of a computer key. Take that, you robots. High score!

Afterword

The Constant Is Change

With the advent of the Web, any semblance of quiescence and constancy vanished from the reference desk. In the late 1990s, the Web gave us such a myriad of resources that we couldn't keep track of them all. In the postmillennial dot-com meltdown, many of these free services have disappeared. Still, strong companies survived merely annealed by the turbulent process. The new century has been a fresh formation of online riches. Yes, the surface of the open Web still glints with information jewels that are there for the taking. You only need to know where to look for them.

The Internet is no utopia. But it is still a great place to shop—for bargain reference resources!

About the Author

Irene E. McDermott is a Reference Librarian and the Systems Manager at the San Marino Public Library in California. Before she received her library degree from UCLA, McDermott served as Associate Research Editor for Salem Press for more than 10 years. During that time, she worked at night to hone her skills as an actress, comedienne, and theatrical director. McDermott abandoned theater for a career as an information professional when she became excited by the possibilities of the emerging World Wide Web. McDermott lives in Pasadena with her husband and son. Her column, "Internet Express," appears monthly in *Searcher* magazine.

Index

B

C

D

G

games, 82–86
Gardner, David, 141
Gardner, Tom, 141
Garriga, "Pirate Pete," 266
GE Center for Financial Learning, 142
genealogy resources, 23, 24–26
Genealogy.com, 26
GeneaNet: Genealogical Database Network, 25–26
General Services Administration, U.S., 235
Georgetown University Health Policy Institute, 125
GetConnected, 155
Giant AntiSpyware, 251
GIFWorks, 211–212
Gigablast, 12
Global Reach, 236
GlobalSCAPE, Inc., 214
glossaries, 192–103, 227
Glossary of WWW, Web Searching, and Netscape Jargon, 193
GMail, 172
Go.com, 7
Goffe, Bill, 63
Google
    beginnings, 8
    Book Search, 112–113
    Earth, 9
    GMail, 172
    Groups, 23–24
    Local Search, 9, *10*
    News, 37
    plans, 2
    relevance rankings, 8
    Scholar, 16, 110
    Toolbar, 244
    Wireless, 235–236
Google Hacks (Calishain), 270
Google Power (Sherman), 17–18
Gookin, Dan, 244
Gould, Stephen Jay, 115–116

governments, statistics and, 61–62
graphic elements, 221
GraphicConverter, 211
GrayLIT Network, 104
Great Books movement, 91–93
Great Books Online, 94–95
"greater-than" symbols, 202–203
Green, Christopher D., 109
Greenspan, Alan, 133
grocery coupons, 158–159
Gronich, Bruce, 216
Gruwell, Cindy A., 186

H

Hacken, Richard, 107
Halsall, Paul, 107
Hanover, University of, Germany, 23
Hardin MD, 67, 121
Harmon, Amy, 161
Harold B. Lee Library, 107
Harrow, Jeffrey R.
The Harrow Technology Report, 267
Hart, Michael S., 92, 111
Hausherr, Tilman, 215
Hawthorn, Nathaniel, 100
Haynes, Craig, 117, 129
Headbone, 84
Headbone Zone Chat, 180–181
Healan, Mike, 252
Health Insurance Consumer Guidelines, 125
Health On the Net Foundation, 130
HealthWeb, 67, 121
hearing impairments, 220, 237
Hearst Communications, 135
Hedley, Jonathan, 215
Heim, Judy, 237
help desks, troubleshooting and, 240
Henderson, John R., 190

HerbMed, 125
"High Flight" (Magee), 9
HighWire Press, 111
HijackThis, 250
Historical Documents, U.S., 108
history
    the law and, 105–109
    subject portals, 79–80
Holy CSS, Zeldman!, 224
Holznagel, Fritz, 29
Home Page Reader, 228
homework help, 73–82
Hoover's Online, 62, 143, *144*
Hornbeck, Jack, 86
Horton, Sarah, 200, 207
Hot Neuron LLC, 111
Hotmail, 167, 168, 171
Houghton Mifflin Company, 80
Housecall, 240–241, *241*
How Things Work, 78
Howe, Eric, 248
Howes, Eric L., 252
HowStuffWorks, 78, 197
HTML Cheatsheet, 206
HTML Creator, 208
HTML editors, 207–208
HTML (hyper-text markup
    language)
    colors choice, 208–210
    description, 202–205
    references, 205–207
    use of, 199–200
HTML Tidy Online, 215
HTML Tutor, 206
HTML Writers Guild, 226
Human-Computer Interaction Lab
    (HCIL), 80
Human Rights Library, 107
humanities, subject portals, 60
Humanities Text Initiative, 101
HumanWare, 233
Humbul Humanities Hub, 60
Hutchins, Robert Maynard, 91
Hylton, Jeremy, 100
HyperHistory Online, 79

hyperlinks
    invention of, 1
    verifying, 215

I

IAF, searching, 23
Iannuzzi, Patricia, 189
IBM Accessibility Center, 222, 228
ICANN (Internet Corporation for
    Assigned Names and
    Numbers), 30–31
iCivilEngineer, 65
ICQ (I seek You), 180
ICyouSee, 190, *191*
IE-SPYAD, 252
Illinois, University of, 92, 121, 229
image editors, 210–212
ImageJ, 211
Indiana University, 99
InfiniteChat, 180
INFO TO GO, 273
Infogrip, 232
Infomine, 58
Infomotions, Inc, 95
InFoPeople, 192
information, access methods, 240
Information Please, 74–75
Information Technology Access
    Rehabilitation Engineering
    Research Center, 230
Information Today, Inc., 273
Infoseek, history, 7
InfoSpace.com, 21
InfoUSA, 22
Inktomi, history, 10
Inomics, 63
instant messaging (IM), 179–180
Institute for Learning and
    Research Technology, 61
InteliHealth, 124
Intelius People Search, 27–28
Internet Classics Archive, 99

T

More Great Books from Information Today, Inc.

The Accidental Library Manager

By Rachel Singer Gordon

In *The Accidental Library Manager*, Rachel Singer Gordon provides support for new managers, aspiring managers, and those who find themselves in unexpected management roles. Gordon fills in the gaps left by brief and overly theoretical library school coursework, showing library managers how to be more effective in their positions and how to think about their work in terms of the goals of their larger institutions. Included are insights from working library managers at different levels and in various types of libraries addressing a wide range of management issues and situations.

384 pp/softbound/ISBN 1-57387-210-5 $29.50

The NextGen Librarian's Survival Guide

By Rachel Singer Gordon

Here is a unique resource for next generation librarians, addressing the specific needs of GenXers and Millenials as they work to define themselves as information professionals. The book focuses on how NextGens can move their careers forward and positively impact the profession. Library career guru Rachel Singer Gordon—herself a NextGen librarian—provides timely advice along with tips and insights from dozens of librarians on issues ranging from image to stereotypes, to surviving library school and entry-level positions, to working with older colleagues.

2006/240 pp/softbound/ISBN 1-57387-256-3 $29.50

The Accidental Webmaster

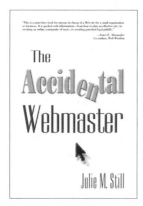

By Julie M. Still

Here is a lifeline for the individual who has not been trained as a Webmaster, but who—whether by choice or under duress—has become one nonetheless. While most Webmastering books focus on programming and related technical issues, *The Accidental Webmaster* helps readers deal with the full range of challenges they face on the job. Author, librarian, and accidental Webmaster Julie Still offers advice on getting started, setting policies, working with ISPs, designing home pages, selecting content, drawing site traffic, gaining user feedback, fundraising, avoiding copyright problems, and much more.

208 pp/softbound/ISBN 1-57387-164-8 $29.50

The Accidental Systems Librarian

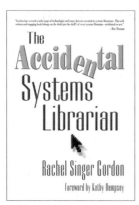

By Rachel Singer Gordon
Forword by Kathy Dempsey

Author Rachel Singer Gordon believes that anyone with a solid foundation in the practices and principles of librarianship and a willingness to confront changing technology can serve effectively in a library technology position—with or without formal computer training. Gordon's advice on using research, organizational, and bibliographic skills to solve various systems problems helps "accidental" systems librarians develop the skills they need to succeed. This is an important book for any librarian who wants to deal more effectively with technology in her or his institution.

288 pp/softbound/ISBN 1-57387-161-3 $29.50

The New OPL Sourcebook

By Judith A. Siess

This updated and expanded edition of the essential guide for small and one-person libraries (Opls) covers virtually every key management topic of interest to OPLs. In addition to offering a wealth of practical tips, strategies, and case studies, author Judith Seiss takes an international perspective that reflects the growing number of OPLs worldwide. The book's in-depth Resources section lists important organizations, publications, vendors and suppliers, discussion lists, and Web sites.

2006/464 pp/softbound/ISBN 1-57387-241-5 $39.50

The Successful Academic Librarian

By Gwen Meyer Gregory

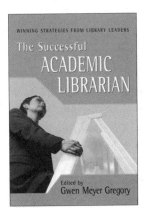

The role of academic librarian is far from cut-and-dried. For starters, there are the numerous job classifications: staff or professional employment, full faculty status, various forms of tenure, continuing contract, and/or promotion through academic ranks. While every academic librarian works to meet the research needs of faculty and students, many are expected to assume other obligations as part of a faculty or tenure system. If this were not enough to test a librarian's mettle, the widely varying academic focuses and cultures of college and university libraries almost certainly will. This book, expertly edited by academic librarian, writer, and speaker Gwen Meyer Gregory, is an antidote to the stress and burnout that almost every academic librarian experiences at one time or another. Gregory and nearly 20 of her peers and mentors take a practical approach to a full range of critical topics facing the profession.

256 pp/hardbound/ISBN 1-57387-232-6 $39.50

The Extreme Searcher's Internet Handbook

By Randolph Hock

This is the essential guide for anyone who uses the Internet for research—librarians, teachers, students, writers, business professionals, and others who need to search the Web proficiently. Randolph (Ran) Hock covers strategies and tools (including search engines, directories, and portals) for all major areas of Internet content. Readers with little to moderate searching experience will appreciate Hock's helpful, easy-to-follow advice, while experienced searchers will discover a wealth of new ideas, techniques, and resources. Anyone who teaches the Internet will find this book indispensable.

296 pp/softbound/ISBN 0-910965-68-4 $24.95

Yahoo! to the Max

By Randolph Hock

With its many and diverse features, it's not easy for any individual to keep up with all that Yahoo! has to offer. Fortunately, Ran Hock—"The Extreme Searcher"—has created a reader-friendly guide to his favorite Yahoo! tool for online research, communication, investment, e-commerce, and a range of other useful activities. In *Yahoo! to the Max*, Ran helps Web users take advantage of many of Yahoo!'s most valuable offerings—from its portal features, to Yahoo! Groups, to unique tools some users have yet to discover. As with all Extreme Searcher guides, the author's regularly updated Web page helps readers stay current on the new and improved Yahoo! features he recommends.

256 pp/softbound/ISBN 0-910965-69-2 $24.95

Super Searchers Go to School

By Joyce Kasman Valenza

Edited by Reva Basch

Twelve prominent K–12 educators and educator-librarians share their techniques and tips for helping students become effective, life-long information users. Through a series of skillful interviews, Joyce Kasman Valenza—techlife@school columnist for the *Philadelphia Inquirer* and herself a tech-savvy high school librarian—gets the experts to reveal their field-tested strategies for working with student learners and educator peers. You'll discover techniques for teaching search tool selection, evaluating result lists and Web sites, deciding when to use a professional database or the Invisible Web, and much more.

272 pp/softbound/ISBN 0-910965-70-6 $24.95

Best Technology Practices in Higher Education

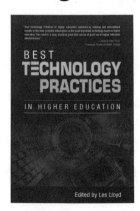

Edited by Les Lloyd

A handful of progressive teachers and administrators are integrating technology in new and creative ways at their colleges and universities, raising the bar for all schools. Editor Les Lloyd (*Teaching with Technology*) has sought out the most innovative and practical examples in a range of key application areas, bringing together more than 30 technology leaders to share their success stories. The book's 18 chapters include firsthand accounts of school technology projects that have transformed classrooms, services, and administrative operations.

264 pp/hardbound/ISBN 1-57387-208-3 $39.50

The Web Library
Building a World Class Personal Library with Free Web Resources

By Nicholas G. Tomaiuolo
Edited by Barbara Quint

With this remarkable, eye-opening book and its companion Web site, Nicholas G. (Nick) Tomaiuolo shows how anyone can create a comprehensive personal library using no-cost Web resources. *The Web Library* provides a wealth of URLs and examples of free material you can start using right away, but, best of all, it offers techniques for finding and collecting new content as the Web evolves.

440 pp/softbound/ISBN 0-910965-67-6 • $29.95

The Information Professional's Guide to Career Development Online

By Sarah L. Nesbeitt and Rachel Singer Gordon

This book is designed to meet the needs of librarians interested in using online tools to advance their careers. It offers practical advice on topics ranging from current awareness services and personal Web pages to distance education, electronic resumes, and online job searches. New librarians will learn how to use the Internet to research education opportunities, and experienced info pros will learn new ways to network.

416 pp/softbound/ISBN 1-57387-124-9 $29.50

B' :   ᵍue
U   've   Un'